5x   10/2010   10/11. 6x

East Meadow Public Library
1886 Front Street
East Meadow, New York 11554
516-794-2570
www.eastmeadow.info

Young Adult

Authors of **Banned Books**

J. K. Rowling
Banned, Challenged, and Censored

Joan Vos MacDonald

Enslow Publishers, Inc.
40 Industrial Road
Box 398
Berkeley Heights, NJ 07922
USA
http://www.enslow.com

Library of Congress Cataloging-in-Publication Data

MacDonald, Joan Vos.
    J.K. Rowling : banned, challenged, and censored / Joan Vos MacDonald.
        p. cm. — (Authors of banned books)
    Includes bibliographical references and index.
    ISBN-13: 978-0-7660-2687-2
    ISBN-10: 0-7660-2687-6
        1. Rowling, J. K.—Criticism and interpretation—Juvenile literature. 2. Rowling, J. K.—Censorship—Juvenile literature. 3. Children's stories, English— History and criticism—Juvenile literature. 4. Potter, Harry (Fictitious character)—Juvenile literature. 5. Challenged books—Juvenile literature. 6. Prohibited books—Juvenile literature. 7. Censorship—Juvenile literature. I. Title. II. Series.
    PR6068.O93Z763 2006
    823'.914—dc22

                                                                        2006015874

Printed in the United States of America

10 9 8 7 6 5 4 3 2 1

To Our Readers: This book has not been authorized by J. K. Rowling or her agents or assigns, including Warner Bros. Entertainment, Inc. Harry Potter is a trademark of Warner Bros. Entertainment, Inc.

We have done our best to make sure that all Internet addresses in this book were active and appropriate when we went to press. However, the author and publisher have no control over and assume no liability for the material available on those Internet sites or on other Web sites they may link to. Any comments or suggestions can be sent by e-mail to comments@enslow.com or to the address on the back cover.

♻ Enslow Publishers, Inc., is committed to printing our books on recycled paper. The paper in every book contains 10% to 30% post-consumer waste (PCW). The cover board on the outside of each book contains 100% PCW. Our goal is to do our part to help young people and the environment too!

Contents

These Harry Potter fans came to a bookstore in Hogwarts robes with glasses and forehead scars; one even had his own version of Hedwig, the owl.

Chapter 1

The Controversy Surrounding Harry Potter

Spending an hour on a slowly snaking bookstore line was not really difficult for Pilar Mendez-Cruz, eleven, as long as she kept her eyes on the prize. Waiting with her fellow fans meant that Pilar would be the 146th person in that store to buy *Harry Potter and the Half-Blood Prince* when the sixth book in the J. K. Rowling series officially went on sale at midnight. This was the second time that Pilar had waited on a bookstore line for a midnight Harry Potter sale. While waiting for this one, she might take part in such Potter events as wizard wand making, knitting a scarf with the colors of Potter's school-house, magic shows, and Harry Potter look-alike and trivia contests.[1]

Dressed for the occasion in a rubber pair of trademark Potter glasses, Pilar said she started reading the series because all her friends liked the books so much. At first, her mother had to read them to her, but by the time the fourth book came out, she could read it herself—and had become a self-described "fanatic."

"Sometimes it feels like I am there," said Pilar enthusiastically. "The magic is really nice. It's somewhere different."

Pilar thinks the books helped improve her reading skills, as she would look over her mother's shoulder while she was reading the books. "They [her parents] didn't know I needed glasses so I was behind in my reading," she said, "but I wanted to read the books so much I caught up."[2]

At seventeen, Amanda Javaly is a year older than Harry Potter, and she feels like she has grown up with him. That is one reason she waited so patiently on the same bookstore line for her copy of the new book.

"Harry is a normal kid. He could be one of us and yet he exists in a different dimension," said Amanda, who wore a replica of Harry's school robes while she waited on line to make a wand at the bookstore party.

Amanda began reading the books in middle school, and her interest has not lagged.

"His life is different from ours, and yet it's the same. He's a wizard and yet he's a whiny teenager. Everyone goes to school, but it's cool trying to think of how to get to station platform nine and three quarters," she said of the magical train platform from which the

Hogwarts Express leaves to take Harry to Hogwarts School of Witchcraft and Wizardry.

Although Amanda has heard that Rowling's books have been challenged and banned in schools and even burned in bonfires, she wonders, "Why do people care? Why can't we fantasize as long as we know it's not real?"[3]

Harry Potter Goes to School

As a fourth-grade teacher, Lin Butter knows all about the controversy J. K. Rowling's books can cause, but she was surprised when it happened in her upstate New York school district.

The school superintendent had to reassign a child from her class because Butter was using the Potter books as a teaching tool. The child's parent said Butter was using the books to promote the devil.

"Harry is a normal kid. He could be one of us and yet he exists in a different dimension."

Butter started using the books five years ago with a class she taught for both third and fourth grades. They covered the first five books in the series.

"I chose the books because they were so extraordinarily well written and they get kids into reading," said Butter, who figured she would skip sleeping the night the sixth book came out so she could have a copy to take on her vacation the next morning.

Butter also likes to use the books in class because they deal with the battle between good and evil and cover philosophical issues.

"They do have their dark side, but the books deal well with the choices that kids are going to have to make in their lives—what you will support, what's real in your life," she said.[4]

Although the school district Butter teaches in reassigned the student whose parents objected, they supported her decision to use the books as teaching tools. That has not always been the case when J. K. Rowling's books were used in classroom settings.

A few days before the release of the sixth book, an elementary school in Skellingthorpe, England, canceled a planned Harry Potter Day because a minister complained that the school's headmaster was leading "children into areas of evil."[5]

There have been many cases of similar events being canceled in the United States—and also many instances of the books being withdrawn from school curriculums and libraries. Although many teachers, librarians, and parents have praised the books for encouraging children to love reading, some concerned parents have prayed over them. Some parents wanted to destroy every copy they could find to protect their children from what they considered a dangerous moral threat.

Even more felt that these books had no place in public schools because they promoted an unhealthy interest in the occult or anything supernatural. A few parents were even motivated to burn the books.

Shortly before the 2007 publication of the seventh and final book in the series, *Harry Potter and the Deathly Hallows*, the dangers of the wizarding world Rowling has created were still being debated in court. In a Georgia state courthouse, Laura Mallory, a mother of four, fought to have the books banned from Gwinnett County school libraries and classrooms because, she said, "witchcraft is a religion practiced by some people and, therefore, the books should be banned because reading them in school violates the constitutional separation of church and state."

The Georgia State Department of Education initially refused to remove the books. So Mallory appealed to the Gwinnett Superior Court, which upheld the earlier education department decision, saying that the books could remain on school library bookshelves. Mallory had first challenged the books two years earlier when they were used as part of a lesson in one of her children's classes.[6]

Burning and Banning Books

Only six weeks after the enthusiastically received publication of *Harry Potter and the Order of the Phoenix* in 2003, the members of the Jesus Non-Denominational Church in Greenville, Michigan, decided to publicly demonstrate their concern by gathering around a bonfire with their copies of the book.[7]

They were not gathering to watch a mythical phoenix bird rise from the ashes—as happens in this book—but to watch scorched remnants of the books' pages dance in the fire's heat.

Members of this and other churches made a statement that year by burning Harry Potter books, as well as other books, magazines, and music CDs. In the Middle Ages, when actual copies of books were rare, burning books served as an effective way to silence the ideas in them. Today, with bookstore shelves brimming, book burnings can't aim to get rid of offending books entirely, but they do make a statement.

The concerned church members surrounding the bonfire wanted to state that J. K. Rowling, the author of Harry Potter, does not share their values and that she promotes a dangerous point of view. By making the occult so attractive to young people, they say the books could turn young impressionable minds away from everything they have been raised to believe.

"We at Jesus Non-Denominational Church refuse to allow Satan to take the minds of our children," said Pastor Tommy Turner. "We will do all that is in us to stand and hold up a standard of righteousness and we will win."[8]

Although J. K. Rowling claims her wizarding world is purely imaginary and that she doesn't believe in the kind of magic found in her books, for some parents, the magic found in the Harry Potter book series makes them the most dangerous set of books to be released this century.

Burning is not the only danger these books have faced. They have been challenged so many times that

10

the books have repeatedly topped the most frequently challenged book lists created by the American Library Association (ALA).

Who Decides What You Read?

The author of these controversial books finds the idea of censorship to be deeply offensive and, when it applies to Harry Potter books, very misplaced.

"I personally think they're very mistaken," said Rowling of one attempt to remove her books from a school library in Santa Fe, New Mexico. "What scares me is these people are trying to protect children from their own imagination. It's my profound belief that there's a tendency to underestimate children on all sorts of levels."[9]

While she says that parents have the right to decide what their children read, she thinks their fear of her books is misguided—and their attempts to keep other people's children from reading her books is dangerous.

Not Everyone Is Wild About Harry

In some circles, the name Harry Potter is spoken of with the same sort of fear and loathing the students at Hogwarts might reserve for his enemy, the evil wizard Lord Voldemort.

According to the ALA, in 2004 alone, there were twenty-six challenges to remove the books from library shelves in sixteen states. Altogether, the books have been challenged seventy-one times in twenty-one different school districts in Texas alone.[10]

Attempts have been made to have the book banned from school curriculums, to restrict access to them in school libraries, and to have the books removed from school libraries altogether.

"What scares me is these people are trying to protect children from their own imagination," says one librarian.

The parents who believe that Harry Potter is a threat have a right to be concerned about what their children read and, as parents, to monitor influences their children are exposed to. But do they have the right to determine what can and what cannot be taught in schools or restrict other children's access to books? Some people say this is an issue that involves a right guaranteed by the First Amendment to the U.S. Constitution.

Protecting Children or Protecting Children's Rights?

The First Amendment to the U.S. Constitution states:

> Congress shall make no law respecting an establishment of religion, or prohibiting the free exercise thereof; or abridging the freedom of speech, or of the press; or the right of the people peaceably to assemble, and to petition the Government for a redress of grievances.

Having access to information is considered to be part of the rights that fall under the "freedom of speech or of the press" part of the amendment, but how the authors of the Constitution meant to apply it has often been reinterpreted.

Does a parent's desire to protect a child override the right to freedom of expression and access to the ideas presented in books, newspapers, and other forms of media? Because new situations prompt new interpretations of the First Amendment, it continues to be discussed and debated. For example, how does it affect new mediums of communication never imagined by the men who wrote the Constitution—such as television, movies, and the Internet?

Are You Old Enough for Hogwarts?

Age is a factor in deciding what is appropriate. While children technically have many of the same First Amendment rights under the Constitution that adults do, exceptions are made to protect them. The law allows parents to make most decisions for minors as long as they are considered to be fit parents. This is particularly true in terms of what children may read, the films they may see, and the music they may listen to. One example in which the rights of children are restricted in the interest of protecting them is pornography. Adults may view pornographic materials as part of their First Amendment rights, but pornographic material may not be marketed to minors.

Not only are many books written for adults not suitable for children, but a book written for a middle-school student may not be appropriate for a first grader. Is it right for schools to restrict access to books they consider children too young for—and who decides what age is too young? If so, what are the criteria by which such a book can be judged? Are certain subjects completely off limits for younger children? Can a book be too sophisticated, too dark, or too violent for a child, and, if so, at what age do such criteria apply?

Although her books are about children and young adults, Rowling has said that she never wrote the books with eight-year-olds in mind. Eight or nine is the youngest she would advise reading the books, even though she has broken her own rule by reading them with her daughter.

"I do have parents coming up to me and saying, 'He's six and he loved your book,'" said Rowling. "Well that's great but I know what's coming, and I think six is a tiny bit too young."

With a younger child, Rowling advises reading the books together so you can discuss them. She never planned to read the books to her daughter, Jessica, until she was seven. But when Jessica started school at six and everyone else knew all about Harry Potter but her, Rowling began reading the books to her. Jessica became a big fan.[11]

As the series progresses and Harry grows up, the books grow darker and more adult. Readers are faced with increasingly serious and complex subjects, such as the existence of evil and the reality of death. Younger readers may benefit from adult guidance.

The Role of Librarians

Parents have complained that it is hard to protect their children from inappropriate books when the books in question are in a library and children may take them out without supervision. Should librarians get involved in deciding what individual children should read? Librarians often find themselves in the middle of book-banning controversy, caught between a desire to help parents protect their children and a desire to uphold the First Amendment.

On June 30, 1972, the American Library Association adopted a new policy called Free Access to Libraries for Minors: An Interpretation of the Library Bill of Rights. The policy states:

> The rights of an individual to the use of a library should not be denied or abridged because of his age. . . .The American Library Association holds that it is the parent— and only the parent—who may restrict his children—and only his children—from access to library materials and services. The parent who would rather his child not have access to certain materials should so advise the child.[12]

That means that a librarian cannot act in place of a parent. He or she cannot presume how a parent might feel about the moral value of a particular book and thereby restrict a child's access to that book.

This policy statement also applies to school librarians. Some librarians, especially in small communities, may personally disagree with this policy, while some must face pressure from the community—parents, the school board—to remove or restrict certain books.

Banning Books in Schools

Librarians are not the only officials making decisions about which books should be available in school libraries. In November 1999, Gary Feenstra, the superintendent of schools in Zeeland, Michigan, read the first Harry Potter book and decided to remove it from library shelves, bypassing his school district's process for challenging books. He decided to restrict children's access because, he said, he was protecting the rights of those whose religious views might be offended.[13] Teachers were also not allowed to read the book aloud during classes.[14]

Mary Dana, a teacher, and Nancy Zennie, a parent with two children in the school district, started a campaign to overturn the restrictions and organized Muggles for Harry Potter, which became a national group focusing on First Amendment rights issues for children. Because of the opposition to the restrictions, the school formed a committee of parents and school district employees and voted to reduce the restrictions.[15]

Eventually, Superintendent Feenstra agreed to put the books back in the elementary and middle schools,

16

This family dressed as characters from the Harry Potter books for a program at the library. While many librarians and teachers have been happy about how the Rowling books have encouraged children to read, some people have objected to what they see as harmful content.

to permit readings in middle schools, and to let children use the series in book reports. In elementary schools, teachers may not read them aloud, but students can take books from the library.[16]

More Controversy

Critics of the Harry Potter series are not only concerned about the occult; they mention an inappropriate amount of violence and dark themes unsuitable for young children. They also feel the books promote disrespect of adults.

Using Harry Potter in the curriculum is also frowned on because some parents believe it promotes the religion of Wicca, a nature-based religion, through an association with witchcraft. According to the U.S. Constitution, no religion should be promoted over another in public schools.

In one such case, Tony Leanza, a minister at the New Wine Christian Center in York, Pennsylvania, asked for the books to be banned in schools because Wicca was a religion and promoting it violates the separation of church and state guaranteed by the U.S. Constitution.[17] His mission was not successful, and the schools retained the books without restriction.

To date, no challenge that aimed to ban the Potter books has ever been permanently successful.

Parents for and Against Potter

For the parents who want to keep their children safe from what they believe are inappropriate stories, this has been a frustrating experience. For Harry Potter fans, the concern voiced by these parents is puzzling. For many of the parents of these fans, the movement to exclude a book that actually gets children excited about reading is a bad idea.

"You can't ask for a better poster child against censorship than Harry Potter," said Chris Finan, president of the American Booksellers Foundation for Free Expression and sponsor of the Web site Kidspeak. "For Harry Potter to be attacked was an anti-censorship defender's dream."[18] Finan feels that the protests against these well-loved books make the parents who protest against them seem petty and that attacks against the books can help children understand how vulnerable First Amendment rights can be and how important it is to protect these rights.

Parents Against Bad Books in Schools (PABBIS), a Virginia-based organization of concerned parents, disagrees. While the group does feel that parents should have to give their consent if Harry Potter is used in a school curriculum, an unidentified PABBIS spokesperson wrote, "We don't think the Harry Potter series is a good example book for children to understand the issues involved, since the vast majority of controversies about K-12 books do not involve witchcraft/occult."[19] PABBIS is worried that the controversy over the Harry Potter books will distract people from a more significant concern—the number of books found in school libraries that contain what they consider to be an unacceptable level of sex and violence for the age group that is exposed to them.

For people who feel strongly about the freedom of expression, the desire to restrict children's access to books is far more dangerous than what's written in these or any other books. For some parents who want to protect their children, the library may not seem like a safe place to leave them.

Is Harry Potter an enjoyable fantasy or a devious plot to interest children into the occult? The seven-book series has attracted millions of fans but also a few seriously concerned critics. Although there were fewer protests against the books by the time the series was completed, the controversy may continue.

Chapter 2

Banned, Censored, and Bowdlerized

How many previously banned children's books have you read and considered harmless? You may be surprised to find that many children's and young adult classics, as well as fairy tales and comic books, have been challenged, censored, or had portions deleted in schools across the country.

The list of banned books includes such favorites as *The Lion, the Witch and the Wardrobe* by C. S. Lewis, *The Wizard of Oz* by L. Frank Baum, *A Light in the Attic* by Shel Silverstein, *A Wrinkle in Time* by Madeline L'Engle, *Charlie and the Chocolate Factory* by Roald Dahl, *The Diary of Anne Frank, Little House on the Prairie* by Laura Ingalls Wilder, *Adventures of Huckleberry Finn* by Mark Twain, *In the Night Kitchen* by Maurice Sendak, and *Are You There God? It's Me, Margaret,* as well as several other Judy Blume books.

21

What's Wrong With These Books?

Like the Harry Potter books, *The Lion, the Witch and the Wardrobe, The Wizard of Oz,* and *A Wrinkle in Time* were challenged because they were said to encourage interest in the occult. *A Light in the Attic* and *Charlie and the Chocolate Factory* were considered to be disrespectful to adults. Parents objected to Maurice Sendak's *In the Night Kitchen* because of its "gratuitous nudity"—the book's hero did not wear pants in one picture.[1]

The Diary of Anne Frank was challenged for several reasons, including one complaint by the Alabama Textbook Committee about it being "a real downer."[2] Judy Blume's books have often been challenged because of their frank references to controversial subjects such as an adolescent's awakening interest in sex.[3]

Books have been challenged because they represent certain groups of people—women, American Indians, African Americans—in what some consider an unfair or disrespectful light, even if the portrayal is limited to a single character or is considered historically accurate in the context of the time in which the story is set.

For example, *Little House in the Big Woods* was removed from one third-grade classroom, and *Little House on the Prairie* was challenged in one elementary school, because some readers say they portray American Indians negatively.[4]

Adventures of Huckleberry Finn has been repeatedly challenged because it is said to be demeaning to African Americans. It uses the word *nigger*—even though the story does not endorse slavery or any oppression of

African Americans, and, in fact, has a strong, antiracist message for the time it was written.[5]

Shakespeare's play *The Merchant of Venice* was banned from a Michigan classroom in 1980 for its negative, and some say stereotypical, portrayal of the Jewish character, Shylock.[6]

Fairy tales such as "Little Red Riding Hood," "Cinderella," "Jack and the Beanstalk," and "Beauty and the Beast" have been accused by the Council on Interracial Books as portraying women as weak and waiting to be rescued.[7]

Is Editing Censorship?

In some cases, it might seem to be a simple solution to remove an offending word or delete some paragraphs, but who decides what to remove, and how does this affect the literary content of a book or the point an author is trying to make?

In 1807, a man named Thomas Bowdler and his sister Henrietta Bowdler published their *Family Shakespeare*. In this version of Shakespeare's works, more than one hundred references to sex as well as potentially controversial religious references were removed. As a result, the word *bowdlerized* is now used to refer to the act of deleting offensive words or passages in a written work. Books bowdlerized for children and young adults include versions of *Gulliver's Travels*, Uncle Remus stories, *The Adventures of Tom Sawyer*, Grimm's fairy tales, and some Hans Christian Anderson fairy tales.

The Temperature at Which Books Burn

If you really want to know how bad it might be to remove a few offensive words, ask an author.

Ray Bradbury is a science-fiction writer whose book *Fahrenheit 451,* a novel about censorship, is so named because that's the temperature at which paper is said to burn. Bradbury says,

> There is more than one way to burn a book. And the world is full of people running around with lit matches. Every minority, be it Baptist/Unitarian, Irish/Italian/ Octogenarian/ Zen Buddhist, Zionist/Seventh-day Adventist, Women's Lib/Republican, Mattachine/ Four Square Gospel feels it has the will, the right, the duty to douse the kerosene, light the fuse.[8]

The book-burning quote was part of a short essay that Bradbury added to his book when it was reissued. He wrote it because he was furious that a publisher asked to include one of his stories in a school text-book—if only two worrisome phrases could be deleted. Bradbury said no, seeing the deletions as a form of unacceptable censorship. The deletions amounted to five words. It was the principle of the thing, said Bradbury.

"Most people who try to remove books really are well-meaning and they're very concerned about the information that's being made available to children and young people," said Judith Krug, who is director of the Office for Intellectual Freedom. "But they're also smart enough to realize that their views of the world, their value systems, are going to be much safer and more readily believed if there's no opposition to them."[9]

The History of Censorship

There is nothing new about censorship or about the desire to protect impressionable minds—both are older than books as we know them.

In 387 B.C., Plato suggested that Homer's works the *Iliad* and the *Odyssey* were not suitable for young readers. A few centuries later, the Roman emperor Caligula tried to ban the *Odyssey* because he worried

There is nothing new about censorship or about the desire to protect impressionable minds—both are older than books as we know them.

that the Greek ideals portrayed in the story would lead his people to revolt.[10]

The word *censor* comes from a Latin word meaning "to form an opinion." In those days, public officials named censors counted the number of people through a census, but they could also ban people for writing an immoral book.

Twenty years after Johann Gutenberg invented the printing press in 1450, the first popular books were printed in Germany, and within another twenty years, the first censorship office was established.

During the reign of King Henry VIII of England (1509 to 1547), all printers were required to submit manuscripts to the Church of England for approval before they could be released, and imported publications were banned.

The astronomer Galileo was put under house arrest in Italy from 1633 until his death in 1641 because he dared to print a book that said the earth revolved around the sun, which was then contrary to the teachings of the Roman Catholic Church.

Throughout history, most banned or challenged books have offended in one of three ways. They were considered blasphemous—showing disrespect for God or religion. They were considered politically dangerous. Or they were morally offensive—having the power to corrupt people's minds or turn them away from traditional values.

Faith, Patriotism, and Morality

The first publication to be banned in the American colonies was a religious pamphlet. In 1650, William Pynchon's *The Meritorious Price of Our Redemption* was confiscated by the Puritan authorities and burned in the Boston Marketplace because authorities found that it contradicted accepted religious beliefs.[11]

In 1872, Anthony Comstock founded the New York Society for the Suppression of Vice. He persuaded Congress to pass a law in 1873 that granted the government the authority to confiscate books thought to be "lewd, indecent, filthy or obscene." The law, which became known as the Comstock Law, was used to confiscate 120 tons of printed works and prosecute 3,500 people. It censored many works now considered classic literature, including books by Ernest Hemingway, John Steinbeck, Victor Hugo, James Joyce, and D. H. Lawrence.

Although the Comstock Law is no longer enforced and parts of the law have been declared invalid, many books, especially textbooks and school library books, are still challenged on moral grounds.

In the 1970s, groups such as Focus on the Family and the American Family Association pressured schools in Texas to remove textbooks with information on subjects such as abortion, out-of-wedlock pregnancy, homosexuality, suicide, drug use, and foul language, which they found damaging to families. According to some groups, textbooks must also be patriotic, which meant they should not be critical of the current government or past actions taken by the government.[12]

Banning books that did not support government policies has also taken place in several countries, including Russia, China, South Africa, and Germany. In 1933, people around the world were shocked when university students in Germany organized a series of burnings of books that Nazi party members found to have an "un-German spirit."

The books burned by the Nazis included those by Albert Einstein, Sigmund Freud, and other well-known thinkers and scientists, many of whom were Jewish.

The Most Frequently Challenged Books of 1990–2000

1. Scary Stories (series) by Alvin Schwartz
2. *Daddy's Roommate* by Michael Willhoite
3. *I Know Why the Caged Bird Sings* by Maya Angelou
4. *The Chocolate War* by Robert Cormier
5. *Adventures of Huckleberry Finn* by Mark Twain
6. *Of Mice and Men* by John Steinbeck
7. Harry Potter (series) by J. K. Rowling
8. *Forever* by Judy Blume
9. *Bridge to Terabithia* by Katherine Paterson
10. Alice (series) by Phyllis Reynolds Naylor [14]

Foreshadowing the Holocaust that was to come, among the writings burned were the works of German poet Heinrich Heine, who said, "Where they burn books, they will in the end, burn human beings too."[13]

Political reasons have motivated the challenging of books in the United States too. When Ray Bradbury first published *Fahrenheit 451* in 1953, a senator from Wisconsin named Joseph McCarthy was hunting anything or anyone associated with communism. McCarthy feared the influence of communism because the United States was engaged in a cold war with the Soviet Union. He wanted to remove all books written by Communists or Communist sympathizers from library shelves. He even objected to the message in Henry David Thoreau's "Essay on Civil Disobedience," which called for American citizens to disobey laws if they felt they were morally wrong. One of the laws Thoreau protested was the right to own slaves, which was legal when the essay was written in 1849. McCarthy wanted to silence anyone who disagreed with him, and in the process he ruined the lives of many people, including Communist party members, people unjustly accused of having Communist sympathies, people who refused to testify against their friends, and people who protested his policies.

That same year, at a graduation ceremony, President Dwight D. Eisenhower cautioned Dartmouth College seniors not to "join the book burners" but to read every book in the library.

"How will we defeat communism," he said, "unless we know what it is, what it teaches and why does it have such an appeal for men, why are so many people swearing allegiance to it?"[15]

Both the parents who complain about books they consider to be inappropriate and the parents who complain that other parents should not be allowed to tell their children what they can read are exercising their right of free speech granted by the First Amendment of the Constitution. Parents exercise that right when they stand up at a school board meeting to challenge a book and ask that it be banned.

When a parent objects to restricting a book by asking a court to decide on its legality, the parent also exercises his or her First Amendment right to free speech. The legal issue at the heart of a book-banning case is whether or not a child's right to access information had been restricted by the removal or restriction of these books.

In 1975, the Island Trees School District in Long Island, New York, removed several books from the school library because they were "anti-American, anti-Christian, anti-Semitic and just plain filthy."[16]

The books included *Go Ask Alice, Soul on Ice, Slaughterhouse-Five, A Hero Ain't Nothing but a Sandwich,*

Church members in Pennsylvania hold a bonfire onto which they throw books, videos, and CDs that they find offensive—including Harry Potter books.

Black Boy, The Fixer, The Naked Ape, Down These Mean Streets, and *The Best Stories of Negro Writers.*

Some students, led by Steven Pico, age seventeen, sued the school board in U.S. District court, claiming that their First Amendment rights had been denied.

The court found in favor of the Island Trees school board and its desire to protect "traditional values." The students then appealed their case to the Second U.S. Circuit Court, which reversed the decision. The school board appealed to the U.S. Supreme Court, which ruled in favor of the students, 5–4. The court ruled that the freedom to express ideas must be supported by the right to receive information and ideas.

President Dwight D. Eisenhower cautioned Dartmouth College seniors not to "join the book burners" but to read every book in the library.

The Supreme Court ruling also said school boards may not remove books because they find them offensive or disagree with the ideas contained in those books. This is the only time the Supreme Court has addressed the question of whether school authorities can remove books from school libraries.[17]

One of the district judges ruling on this case, Judge Mulligan, said that "no matter what choice of books may be made by whatever segment of academe, some other person or group may well dissent."[18]

Steven Pico, the plaintiff in the case, said he learned two things from his time in court. "First, be tolerant of those with whom you disagree; they have a right to hold and espouse beliefs just as you do. And second, never be afraid to confront those who act to limit the freedom of others."[19]

Banning a book does not necessarily keep people from reading it. When Mark Twain found that a library in Massachusetts had banned *Adventures of Huckleberry Finn* in 1885, he wrote to his publisher: "They have expelled Huck from their library as 'trash and suitable only for the slums.' That will sell 25,000 copies for us sure."[20]

Chapter 3

J. K. Rowling:
A Life Worthy of a Novel

Although J. K. Rowling always wanted to be a writer, she never set out to be controversial. If you had told her when she was a college student that she would be a frequently banned author—or even a best-selling author—she might have thought you had an overactive imagination.

The Early Years

A very imaginative child herself, Rowling wrote her first story—about a rabbit who had measles—at the age of six. She created the story to entertain her younger sister, Diana, known as Di. Rowling always wanted to be a writer, but she rarely told anyone.

"I felt very self-conscious about saying that and I came from a family where no one else was a writer or did anything particularly artistic and I think they would have been worried," said Rowling.[1]

J. K. Rowling's real name is Joanne Rowling, but she prefers being called "Jo." Her parents did not actually give her a middle name, but she took the second initial *K* for her favorite grandmother, Kathleen, when she published *Harry Potter and the Sorcerer's Stone.*[2]

On July 31, 1965, Joanne Rowling was born in Cottage Hospital in Yate in Gloucestershire County, in Western England. (Rowling has the same birthday as her hero, Harry Potter.)

When she was born, her parents lived in the nearby town of Chipping Sodbury. Her father, Peter, and her mother, the former Anne Volant, met in 1964 when they were both eighteen. Peter was a member of the British Royal Navy, and Anne was a member of Women's Royal Naval Service, known as the WRENS. The teenagers met on a train from Kings Cross Station in London on its way to Scotland. According to Rowling, her parents said it was love at first sight; the couple married in March of 1965.

Growing Up

Jo Rowling's sister, Diana, was born a year and eleven months after Jo.

"The day of her birth was my earliest memory," said Rowling.[3]

Di was born with her mother's dark hair and brown eyes, and, says Rowling, was the prettier of the two. The sisters spent a lot of time fighting, and Di still has a tiny scar above her eyebrow from one fight in which Jo threw a battery at her.

"The small amount of time we didn't spend fighting, we were the best of friends," said Rowling.[4]

The Rowling family moved twice when Jo was growing up, first to Winterbourne, near Bristol, and then to Tutshill, near Chepstow in Wales. In Winterbourne, there were lots of children to play with, including a brother and sister named Ian and Vikki Potter.[5]

Jo Rowling remembers liking the Potters' last name—and not liking her own at the time—but says she did not base Harry Potter on Ian Potter. As a girl,

As a girl, Rowling says, she was insecure, bookish, and a little bossy, much like the character of Hermione.

Rowling says, she was insecure, bookish, and a little bossy, much like the character of Hermione

When Jo was nine, the Rowling family moved to Tutshill, which was more rural than suburban. Unfortunately, Jo Rowling hated her new school and says she later modeled some of the less likable Hogwarts teachers on teachers in the Tutshill village schools.

While attending the Wydean Comprehensive Secondary School, Rowling had a best friend named Sean Harris. She says she based the character of Ron Weasley on him.[6] He was the only person with whom she ever discussed her desire to be a writer, and he predicted she would be a success. This meant a lot to her.

Harris had a blue and white Ford Anglia car and was one of the first of her friends to have a license. The happy adventures they had driving around in this car inspired her to use the same model car in *The Chamber of Secrets*.

The Difficult Years

During Jo's teenage years, her mother, Anne Rowling, was diagnosed with a quickly progressing form of multiple sclerosis, a degenerative disease of the central nervous system. It was a difficult diagnosis for the whole family to accept.

In 1983, Jo Rowling graduated from Wydean and was accepted into Exeter University, which she chose partly so she could be close to home and her mother. Rather than major in English, she deferred to her parents' wishes and took Greek, Latin, and French, with the idea that she might be able to work as a bilingual secretary after school.

After graduating from Exeter, Rowling moved to London and had a series of jobs. The longest lasting of these jobs was doing office work and research for the human rights organization Amnesty International.[7]

Meeting Harry Potter

In 1990, on what was normally a forty-minute train ride to the northern city of Manchester, a four-hour delay provided enough time for Rowling to dream up a story that would change her life. She visualized a scrawny, black-haired boy with glasses who did not know he was a wizard. In that one train ride, Rowling thought up many of characters that would people his world.

"I had never been so excited about an idea before," said Rowling.[8]

She didn't have a pen, so she just sat and thought about her boy-wizard idea for the whole train ride. That evening, she started working on the first Harry Potter book.

"Harry just sort of strolled into my head ... fully formed," said Rowling.[9] From the beginning she knew the story would not be told in just one book but become a series of seven.[10]

Unfortunately, the year in which Rowling found her inspiration would end badly. On December 30, 1990, her mother died at the age of forty-five. The whole family was stunned and depressed.

About nine months later, partly to escape her deep sense of loss, Jo Rowling took a job teaching English in Oporto, Portugal. There she found the time to write. Her feelings about the loss of her mother found their way into that writing and contributed to the moving descriptions of Harry Potter missing the parents he cannot even really remember.

In her first weeks in Portugal, she wrote the *Sorcerer's Stone* chapter that features the Mirror of Erised. When Harry looks into this magical mirror, he sees his heart's desire—his long-lost parents.

"Not until I'd reread what I'd written did I realize that that had been taken entirely—entirely—from how I felt about my mother's death," said Rowling. "In fact, death and bereavement and what death means, I would say, is one of the central themes in all seven books.[11]

Motherhood and Writing

In Portugal, Rowling met Portuguese journalist Jorge Arantes and married him on October 16, 1992. They had a daughter, Jessica, in 1993. The marriage did not last. In 1994, Rowling and her daughter moved to Edinburgh, Scotland, where her sister lived. Di encouraged her to finish her novel.

While looking for a job that would pay enough to cover suitable child care, Rowling received financial help from the government in the form of monthly unemployment payments. The money she received only covered the bare essentials. To write, Rowling would walk the baby in her stroller until she fell asleep and then sit in Nicolson's Cafe, which was co-owned by her brother-in-law, Roger Moore.[12]

Rowling's plan was to return to teaching. In 1995, she started a teacher certification program and, with some help from a friend, was able to afford the child care she needed. That same year she finished *Harry Potter and the Sorcerer's Stone,* known in England as *Harry Potter and the Philosopher's Stone.*

In mythology, the philosopher's stone is supposed to be able to change less precious metals, such as lead, into precious ones, such as gold, and also to make its

38

owner wiser. When the book was published in the United States, the publisher felt that the American audience might not be as familiar with the story of the philosopher's stone as British readers were and might be more likely to buy a book with a more recognizable magical theme. The titles of books are often changed when they are published in a new country, even if people in both countries speak the same language.

Finding a Publisher

Rowling started out trying to get her book published by sending it to literary agents. These agents read the manuscripts they receive and decide if any of them are worth representing as they are, if they might have potential with some further changes, or if they are not publishable. If an agent decides to represent a book, the agent will send it to people he or she knows in the publishing industry and collects a percentage of the sale price. An agent might reject a book because he or she does not think anyone would buy it, even if the agent personally finds it a good read. Books sent to publishers by literary agents have a greater chance of being published than books sent directly by an author to a publisher.

The first few times that Rowling sent out chapters of the manuscript to literary agents, they were quickly returned. The Christopher Little Agency finally agreed to represent her, but it took them almost a year to find a publisher for the book. According to Rowling's Web site, literary experts working for the publishers that

J. K. Rowling, shown here in a 2000 photo, was astonished by the success of the Harry Potter books as well as the fame they brought her.

received her book did not think it would be a success. One reason given by these experts was that there was no market for such a long children's book. They thought children would not read a book that long. About a dozen publishers decided not to publish it before Bloomsbury Press accepted the book.

That year, Rowling also received a writer's grant from the Scottish Arts Council so she could afford to devote time to writing and still have money to live on. With the grant, Rowling could finally afford to buy a

Literary experts working for the publishers that received Rowling's first book did not think it would be a success. They thought children would not read a book that long.

computer—although she still prefers to write in long-hand. Three days after her novel was published in July 1997, Scholastic Books bid a record-breaking $105,000 to publish the book in the United States. Thanks to word of mouth, the book reached the best-seller lists in about three months.

One reason for the popularity of the books is that they are children's books that can also be enjoyed by adults. The books are well-written, include magical themes—which tend to be popular—and at the same time relate to children's everyday lives. By the time the first book reached the best-seller lists, Rowling was already working on the second novel, *Harry Potter and the Chamber of Secrets,* which was published in the summer of 1998 and shot immediately to the top of the best-seller lists.

The success of her second book meant that Rowling could now afford to write full time, and the books that followed meant that Rowling would probably never have to work at anything else again—unless she wanted to. The third novel, *Harry Potter and the Prisoner of Azkaban,* was published in 1999, *Harry Potter and the Goblet of Fire* in 2000, *Harry Potter and the Order of the Phoenix* in 2003, *Harry Potter and the Half-Blood Prince* in 2005, and *Harry Potter and the Deathly Hallows* in 2007.

Recognition

For her work, Rowling has received many honors, including the Order of the British Empire, given by Queen Elizabeth II of England. Her books have earned children's literature awards including the British Book Awards Children's Book of the Year and the Smarties Prize.

The film rights to the first four Harry Potter books were sold to Warner Brothers, and by 2006, four films had been made. *The Sorcerer's Stone* film was released in 2001, *The Chamber of Secrets* in 2002, *The Prisoner of Azbakan* in 2004, *The Goblet of Fire* in 2005, and *The Order of the Phoenix* in 2007.

Rowling also published two short books based on the Harry Potter series—*Quidditch Through the Ages* (1998) and *Fantastic Beasts and Where to Find Them* (2000), with the proceeds going to one of her favorite charities, Comic Relief. This charity uses comedians to raise awareness of and funds to fight poverty and social injustice in the United Kingdom and Africa. She supports several other charitable causes, including raising money for multiple sclerosis research and the National Council for One Parent Families

On December 26, 2001, Rowling married Dr. Neil Murray; they now live in Scotland. She had a second child, David Gordon Rowling Murray, in March 2003, and a third child, Mackenzie Jean Rowling Murray, in January 2005.[13]

During the final months before the publication of *Harry Potter and the Deathly Hallows*, fans were anxious to know what might happen to the boy wizard. Several books were published that offered predictions, and various Potter-inspired Web sites buzzed with speculation. Rowling had said some of the series' characters would die in the last book, but she would not say if the boy wizard was one. Fans even launched online petitions asking Rowling not to kill off Harry.[14]

Whether Harry lived or died, Rowling said his story would be resolved in the final book of the series— and it was. When she completed the last volume, she had to say a tearful goodbye to the world of wizards and the characters that she had lived with for the last seventeen years.

"I always knew that Harry's story would end with the seventh book, but saying goodbye has been just as hard as I always knew it would be," she said.[15]

The first two days were difficult for Rowling as she mourned the loss of the imaginary world she had loved to retreat to. However, after a week, her sense of loss passed and she felt pleased at the thought of future projects.

"I can write whatever I like, the pressure's off," said Rowling.[16]

Harry Potter and the Deathly Hallows entered *USA Today's* list of best-selling books at No. 1, after selling 8.3 million copies in twenty-four hours in the United States alone. Rowling says her future plans include a book for children and a book for adults, plus possibly a Harry Potter encyclopedia. Odds are, she says, none of her future works could ever be as popular as the Harry Potter books. Nor are any of her future books as likely to be as controversial.[17]

Chapter 4

The Secrets Behind
The Sorcerer's Stone

When readers first meet Harry Potter on the opening pages of *The Sorcerer's Stone,* it is obvious that he has not led a charmed life.

Harry lives with his aunt and uncle, and they wish he didn't. Their two priorities are spoiling their son, Dudley, and keeping their family life as normal as possible—and they know that Harry is not "normal." They know Harry's parents had magical skills and they think that if they don't mention it, there is a chance Harry won't follow the same misguided path. They have told Harry that his parents died in a car crash—not that his parents were murdered by the most evil wizard that ever lived, Lord Voldemort.

Like many orphans in children's literature—Oliver Twist, Cinderella, the Ugly Duckling, the Little Princess—Harry's early life seems very unfair, and he's not appreciated for who he is. He lives in a closet below the stairs, and like Cinderella, he is treated more like a servant than a family member. Like the Ugly Duckling, he will grow up to be something quite different than he seems, something better than he might ever have imagined. He is not an ugly duckling but a swan no one can recognize yet.

Like many heroes in Greek mythology and Arthurian legend, Harry was hidden away until the day it was safe to reveal his true powers.

Although the Dursleys have ignored some random acts of magic on Harry's part, it becomes clear just how different he is when on his eleventh birthday, a blizzard of invitations begin to arrive for Hogwarts School of Witchcraft and Wizardry.

It is easy to feel powerless when you cannot yet make your own decisions—especially if the people making decisions for you do not seem to have your best interests at heart. It can be especially difficult if you do not have a parent or guardian who really loves you for who you are.

Harry is mistreated, and there is nothing he can do to change his life. Anyone who has ever been mistreated or has a keen sense of justice may find it easy to relate to his misfortunes and might applaud his change of fortune when he is invited to attend Hogwarts.

Harry is a likable underdog, and his foster family is so mean that readers root for him to escape their influence. They breathe a sigh of relief when Harry is first invited to Hogwarts, a place where he will finally be appreciated for his special talents.

Harry Arrives at Hogwarts

On his way to school, Harry makes two friends, Ron Weasley, the youngest son of a wizarding family, and

Hermione Grainger, a student whose parents are "Muggles," or not magical. A magical Sorting Hat assigns all three of them to Gryffindor, one of the four houses, or dormitories, at Hogwarts. The other houses are Ravenclaw, Slytherin, and Hufflepuff. Harry also meets a student he doesn't like and who treats him badly. His name is Draco Malfoy, and he is assigned to the house of Slytherin, which is also the former house of Lord Voldemort. The headmaster of Hogwarts, Albus Dumbeldore, is said to be the world's greatest wizard. He is the only one whose powers can match Lord Voldemort's.

Readers breathe a sigh of relief when Harry is first invited to Hogwarts, a place where he will finally be appreciated for his special talents.

Hogwarts is modeled on a British-style boarding school where students usually go to live for the school year. Each house has a common living area and has a housemaster or housemistress to supervise the students. Older students generally have more freedom and some may have limited authority over younger students, as in the case of prefects, or student supervisors. There is usually rivalry between the houses that is often expressed in sporting events.

Hogwarts is more than just a school; it is another world. Like the characters in *The Lion, the Witch and the*

Like the Harry Potter series, the Narnia books appealed to young people's interest in fantasy and adventure. A movie version of the first Narnia book—*The Lion, the Witch and the Wardrobe*—opened in 2005.

Wardrobe and other children's fantasy books, Harry has stepped into a place where all the rules have changed.

At school, Harry studies such subjects as Herbology, the History of Magic, Potions, and Defense Against the Dark Arts. When first taking broom-flying lessons, Harry shows remarkable skill and is asked to join the Gryffindor Quidditch team. (Quidditch is a sport played on broomsticks with flying balls.)

One night, Harry and Ron and Hermione open a door and see a ferocious three-headed dog named Fluffy. They think a mysterious package may be hidden there. Harry finds out that Fluffy belongs to Hagrid, the groundskeeper who has befriended him, and the thing he is guarding has something to do with a man named Nicolas Flamel. The three friends learn that Nicolas Flamel is an alchemist and that the treasure is the Sorcerer's Stone, which can provide wealth and eternal life. Harry, Ron, and Hermione are sure that Lord Voldemort is trying to steal the Sorcerer's Stone. They go to the chamber, lull Fluffy to sleep, and then must play a larger-than-life chess game to get to the place where the stone is hidden. Ron plays brilliantly but is disabled. Hermione's knowledge of potions gets them past another obstacle, but she must return to care for Ron.

Harry encounters one of his teachers, Professor Quirrell, who has been taken over by Lord Voldemort. Harry manages to get the stone. Quirrell/Voldemort tries to kill Harry and get the stone, but Harry's skin blisters him when he touches it. Dumbledore arrives just in time to save Harry. Voldemort slithers away. Dumbledore explains that Quirrell could not touch Harry because of the protective spell of Harry's mother's love when she sacrificed her life for him.

The bravery of Gryffindor's members earns them enough points to rank in first place that year, and Harry goes home knowing the Dursleys will be somewhat kinder to him that summer since they are afraid of him—they don't know he is not allowed to use magic outside school.

A Story of Empowerment

Growing up and becoming more independent can almost seem like you are discovering that you have magical powers that you did not know existed. Adolescence is a time when young people discover they are not helpless but rather beings of tremendous potential and power. Will that power be used for good or evil?

By the end of *The Sorcerer's Stone*, Harry Potter has started to resolve several of the conflicts in his life. First, he lives with relatives who don't like or respect him, but by the end of the first book, they at least fear what he is capable of, which will result in them not being quite so mean to him.

When he first arrives at Hogwarts, Harry worries that he will not fit in, but he makes friends and achieves success. By the end of the book, the members of his house, Gryffindor, have worked so hard and been so brave that they wrestle first place from Slytherin.

The Secrets Behind *The Sorcerer's Stone*

By defeating Lord Voldemort, Harry saves the world of wizards and the world of Muggles from a great evil. He does not want to have to fight evil, but he does, and this makes him a hero in the wizard world.

Through these trials, Harry acquires a better sense of who he is and what he was meant to do in life. He knows that although he may seem a misfit in the Muggle world, there is a place where he can excel.

Rowling has said that the idea of a child who escapes from the confines of the adult world and goes somewhere where he has power, really appealed to her.[1]

Through Harry, Rowling also expresses the yearnings of many children for someone to come along and be able to change the world—to make it safer, more just, kinder.[2]

Growing up is about having more choices—good ones and bad ones. Starting with *Harry Potter and the Sorcerer's Stone,* the series is all about having many choices and how hard it can be to make the right one.

Power is appealing, but is it worth any price? Would you be willing to sacrifice your life to defeat a terrible enemy? Will you believe everything people tell you? When are rules meant to be broken? These are just a few of the questions and choices Harry faces.

The books are also about facing the fact that people are mortal. Harry's parents have died, and, despite the difficulties fate has handed him, he decides he is prepared to face death if that is what it takes to fight Voldemort.

Voldemort seeks the Sorcerer's Stone, which grants the person who owns it immortal life. The book says that you can have immortality, but to obtain it you might have to be evil.[3] Harry chooses good over evil, but it's not always an easy decision. Sometimes he must break rules at school and at home for the greater good. This can be confusing.

Harry's confusion and how he resolves it may help readers understand how they might feel in a similar situation, how people decide what's wrong and what's right when the world of good and evil is not black and white but bewildering shades of gray. Is a person who is bad always going to be bad? Is it okay to be a little bad? Should you fight evil if your life is at risk?

Bruno Bettelheim, an educator and psychiatrist who specialized in child development saw this process as the real value in fairy tales and fantasy stories. In his book *The Uses of Enchantment,* he wrote:

> For a story to truly hold the child's attention, it must entertain him and arouse his curiosity. But to enrich his life, it must stimulate his imagination; help him develop his intellect and to clarify his emotions; be attuned to his anxieties and aspirations; give full recognition to his difficulties, while at the same time ... relate to all aspects of his personality—and this without ever belittling but, on the contrary, giving full credence to the seriousness of the child's predicaments, while simultaneously promoting confidence in himself and in his future.[4]

Does the end justify the means of getting there? The lack of what they see as acceptable morals is a big stumbling block to reading the books, say parents who have challenged them. To them, *Harry Potter and the Sorcerer's Stone* can serve as an instruction manual of violence, disrespect, and murder. Whether this and the other books in the series serve as a mirror for finding full potential or are seen as a way of unleashing evil within, the books do have children reading, thinking, and talking.

Chapter 5

Potter Power

If J. K. Rowling had written one best-selling children's book, she would have considered herself a success beyond her wildest childhood dreams, but she went on to write five more volumes in what she says she has always seen as a seven-part series.

As of July 2007, 325 million Harry Potter books had been sold.[1] By 2005, the books had been translated into sixty-two languages, including Chinese, Czech, Basque, Russian, Portuguese, Norwegian, Latin, and ancient Greek. The Harry Potter books have dished up some potent magic—they have cast a spell that has turned some reluctant readers into bookworms.[2]

Advance orders for the sixth book, *Harry Potter and the Half-Blood Prince,* totaled 2 million.

According to Caroline Horn, *Bookseller* magazine's children's book expert, "There's nothing quite like Harry Potter in publishing."[3]

Harry Potter and the Chamber of Secrets

The second book starts on Harry's birthday, which his family has ignored as usual. During a dinner for guests of Uncle Vernon's, Harry is trying very hard to be quiet but finds a noisy elf named Dobby sitting on his bed. Dobby wants to warn Harry not to go back to Hogwarts because he is in great danger—and in his efforts to warn Harry, he creates chaos at the Dursleys' party.

Harry is picked up by Ron and his twin brothers in a flying car. He is taken to the Weasleys' home, and then he and Ron use the car to go to Hogwarts, where they crash into a tree. During the detention they are given for crashing into the tree and using magic in the Muggle world, only Harry can seem to hear a frightening voice, saying horrible things like "Let me kill you." On Halloween night, Harry hears the voice again, and everyone sees words that say that the chamber of secrets has been opened. Harry finds out that the Chamber of Secrets was built by the founder of the house of Slytherin. Apparently Slytherin's heir will be able to open the chamber, and Harry begins to worry that he might be that heir.

Harry, Ron, and Hermione find a blank book, the diary of a T. M. Riddle. Harry tries writing in it, and Riddle starts writing back. Riddle tells Harry that the Chamber of Secrets has a monster in it and that the young Hagrid was the person who opened it.

Various students—including Hermione—are found petrified. This prompts the Ministry of Magic to arrest Hagrid and remove Dumbledore as headmaster.

Ron and Harry find out that the chamber's monster is a giant snake and that it has taken Ginny Weasley, Ron's little sister. Harry goes to the chamber, where he meets Tom Riddle—who turns out to be the young Hogwarts student who became Lord Voldemort. Harry slays the snake, Ginny awakens, Hagrid is released, and Dumbledore is once more in charge of the school. A potion reverses the petrifying curse, and Hermione is saved.

It turns out that Lucius Malfoy, Draco's father, slipped the troublemaking diary to Ginny and that is what Dobby, his servant, saw. That is why he tried to warn Harry. In gratitude, Harry tricks Malfoy into freeing Dobby. When all is resolved, Harry heads home for another boring summer.

A Dangerous Year at Hogwarts

One important element that is developed in the second book is the prejudice against Muggle-born students at Hogwarts. It becomes more obvious how much the Malfoys and others detest Muggles. This is an important difference between the members of the different houses at Hogwarts.

The "Mudblood–pure blood" controversy in the books makes some people think of the way the Nazis discriminated against the Jews during the Holocaust. It is not such a stretch of the imagination.

"If you think this is farfetched," said Rowling, "look at some of the real charts the Nazis used to determine what consisted of Aryan or Jewish blood."

56

She saw one in the Holocaust Museum after coming up with her Muggle definitions and was chilled to see the Nazis used what she describes as the "same warped logic. It only took one Jewish grandparent to be considered Jewish."[4]

The importance of making a choice between good and evil is explored again in this book. By standing up for Hermione, Ron and Harry show character. By daring to rise above his status as a slave and warn Harry

Shown from left to right are Rupert Grint, Emma Watson, and Daniel Radcliffe, the actors who play best friends Ron, Hermione, and Harry in the movie versions of the Harry Potter books.

of the danger he is in, the house elf Dobby shows again that a character's choices for good—even in the face of great difficulty—have the power to make a difference.

In this book, Harry does not just battle villains outside himself; he must also defeat his own self-doubt. Because he can speak Parselmouth, the language of snakes, and hears the monster's words, "kill, kill, kill," he worries that he too should perhaps

> *The house elf Dobby shows again that a character's choices for good—even in the face of great difficulty—have the power to make a difference.*

be in Lord Voldemort's house, the House of Slytherin. The Sorting Hat almost placed him there instead of Gryffindor. As Dumbledore tells Harry, there is something significant about the fact that Harry instinctively chose not to go to a house with a reputation for abusing magical power, even though he did not know their reputation at the time. Knowing parselmouth does not necessarily mean he is destined to be evil.[5]

Harry Potter and the Prisoner of Azkaban

Critics have described the third book in the series, *Harry Potter and the Prisoner of Azkaban,* as darker and more morally confusing than the earlier books. That could be because Harry is now thirteen, and life gets more confusing as one enters adolescence.

Potter Power

As a person learns more about the world and is exposed to the moral values of others outside his or her family circle, it becomes obvious that everyone does not share the same values. For example, the friends you make might disagree with the values your family holds. A teacher might promote a point of view not shared by the people you have grown up with. Deciding how to feel about certain issues becomes complicated when a person tries to reconcile points of view that may seem to contradict one another. Comparing and questioning values can lead to inner turmoil.

At the start of the third book, Harry is so mad at his Aunt Marge that he inflates her like a balloon and runs away from home. He is picked up by a magic bus, where he hears about an escaped prisoner everyone is afraid of—Sirius Black, who is so famous he has made it into the Muggle news. Black has escaped from Azkaban, the wizarding prison, where he was jailed for murdering thirteen people. No one has ever escaped from Azkaban before, and the wizarding authorities are worried that Black may try to break into Hogwarts.

On the Hogwarts Express, Harry and his friends meet Professor Lupin, their new Defense Against the Dark Arts teacher. The train is searched by cloaked grayish figures known as Dementors, who are the guards at Azkaban. When he sees the Dementors, Harry feels cold and frightened. Lupin gives him some chocolate as a remedy.

Once they get back to Hogwarts, they find that Hagrid has been appointed Care of Magical Creatures teacher. He shows the students how to take care of a hippogriff, a half-horse, half-bird creature named Buckbeak. Harry masters riding it, but Draco Malfoy mishandles it and gets bitten. In Lupin's class, Harry learns how to conjure up a Patronus, a silvery animal shape that acts as a positive force against Dementors.

When the other students are on a field trip to Hogsmeade, a village nearby, Harry sneaks out of Hogwarts. He overhears some teachers discussing Sirius Black; they say that Black tipped off Voldemort as to where Lily and James Potter might be. Black was captured after apparently killing Peter Pettigrew. Harry wants to go after Black, but his friends talk him out of it.

The three friends go to Hagrid's house, where they find Scabbers, Ron's rat, who has escaped; Scabbers bites Ron and bolts. Buckbeak, the hippogriff, is to be executed for biting Malfoy. As they try to catch Scabbers, they see a black dog, who is really Sirius Black. Harry tries to kill him, but Lupin arrives and stops him. Hermione tells them that Lupin is a were-wolf. Lupin explains that Ron's rat, Scabbers, is really Peter Pettigrew.

Lupin says that when his Hogwarts friends Sirius Black, Peter Pettigrew, and James Potter found out he was a werewolf, they also transformed into animals so they could spend time with him when he was transformed. He also says that Pettigrew was actually the one that betrayed the Potters and framed Black. Sirius Black explains that he is Harry's godfather and asks Harry if he would like to live with him; Harry accepts. Harry stops Lupin and Snape from killing Pettigrew because his father would not have wanted it. Pettigrew escapes, and Black is captured by Dementors.

Harry and Hermione realize they must come up with a plan to free Black. She produces a Time-Turner and turns time back to when they were walking to Hagrid's house. They save Buckbeak and use him to rescue Black. At the end of the book, Black, as Harry's godfather, signs a permission slip so he can go leave the school for outings. Harry reasons that having a convicted murderer as a godfather should also be a useful way to frighten the Dursleys.

Life Gets More Complicated

In each book, Harry must fight evil, but in the third book, it is not as simple as it was to tell who the good guys are. It is hard to be sure who is evil and who is not. Sirius Black seems to be evil, but he is not. A rat is really a man who is really a rat. Following the rules is clearly not always the right thing to do, because if Harry had done that, Buckbeak and Black, both innocent, would be dead. It is up to Harry to interpret life's rules and then to reinterpret them.[6]

This book also deals with issues that young adults face, such as controlling anger, facing fears, coping with depression, and learning that being an adult is often different—usually much more complicated—than the way it seems when you are younger.

As Dumbledore says, Harry is vulnerable to the Dementors because of the tragedy he has already faced.

Harry must conjure up a magical positive image to fight off these soul-sucking dark forces.

Something about the frightening lure of the Dementors can be said to be similar to coping with depression. Rowling has said that she was thinking about her own dark days when she created the evil wraiths who suck all happiness out of their victims.[7]

In the third book, it is not as simple as it was to tell who the good guys are. It is hard to be sure who is evil and who is not.

"I don't mean feeling sad," she said. "That is a normal, healthy emotion. Depression is losing the ability to feel certain emotions and one of them is hope."[8]

Harry's emotions take him on a wild ride and sometimes force him to act impulsively. He often acts without thinking about what the result of his actions might be. Harry might have killed Black if he had acted on his rage—the same anger that starts the book when Harry inflates Aunt Marge—but by the end of the book he has learned a lesson about the merits of thinking things through.

By the conclusion of the book, Harry has learned that his father and his father's values live in him, and he can call on them when he needs them. That is a source of great comfort to him.

Chapter 6

Potter's World Becomes Even Darker

J. K. Rowling's fourth Harry Potter book, *Harry Potter and the Goblet of Fire*, is darker yet than the previous three. It starts with the murder of an old man who spies on a conversation between Voldemort and Pettigrew. Harry awakens the next morning from a vivid dream of the incident with his scar burning.

After a visit to the Weasleys' home, Harry and his friends attend the 422nd Quidditch World Cup. At the event, the Dark Mark—a green skull that is the symbol of Voldemort and his supporters, the Death Eaters—appears in the sky.

Back at school, Dumbledore announces that the Triwizard Competition will be held at Hogwarts. The names of champions from three schools of magic are traditionally spit out by a magical Goblet of Fire. Viktor Krum is chosen to represent Durmstrang, and Fleur Delacour represents Beauxbatons. Cedric

Diggory is chosen for Hogwarts, and then the Goblet chooses another name—Harry Potter. Normally, only three students are chosen, and students as young as Harry do not get to compete.

In the first tournament event, the participants must get past a dragon to get a golden egg, and Harry succeeds, tying for first place with Krum. In the second event, with the help of Dobby, Cedric, and a ghost named Moaning Myrtle, Harry dives under the lake and rescues a group of hostages, including Ron, Hermione, Cho Chang, and Fleur's sister. Harry is now tied for first place with Cedric. In the final event of the tournament, Harry succeeds at many spells and tries to save Cedric when Krum sends a curse at him. He also helps Cedric save himself from a huge spider. They decide to share the first prize and each grab a handle of the winning Triwizard Cup. They discover that they have been tricked by Voldermort's supporters. The Triwizard Cup is a Portkey—an everyday object that magically transports them to another place. Once there, a high, cold voice curses Cedric, and he dies. Harry sees Wormtail carrying an ugly thing that is Voldemort. Wormtail cuts Harry and uses his blood to restore Voldemort. Harry and Voldemort duel, and with the help of the ghosts of his parents, he defeats Voldemort and escapes back to Hogwarts with Cedric's body.

It turns out that the Triwizard Tournament was all a ruse to capture Harry for Voldemort. The Minister of Magic refuses to believe that Lord

Voldemort is back or that Harry really saw any of the Death Eaters. Harry knows the battle against evil is far from over and that he will have to fight Voldemort again.

The Battle Against Evil Is Not Easily Fought

In the fourth book, Harry learns that being kind to others has great value and that the battle against evil requires great endurance.

Harry succeeds in the tournament because of his friends. He has been kind to others in the past—Cedric, Moaning Myrtle, Dobby—and they repay that kindness by helping him to accomplish his goals.[1]

Rowling has acknowledged that friendship is very important in the books. But in relationships with other people, there is also the possibility for a great sense of loss if something happens to them.[2] Rowling has said that death and bereavement are a central theme in all seven of her books.[3]

When Cedric dies, Harry also realizes there is a limit to magic, no matter how potent. The price paid in the battle against evil is very high, but there is no alternative to continuing to fight.[4]

Harry Potter and the Order of the Phoenix

In the fifth book, *Harry Potter and the Order of the Phoenix*, Harry is no longer a child, but he is not sure he fits into a world of adults. Hogwarts, the only world Harry has ever felt comfortable in, is often seen as menacing. Even the adults who are not cruel to him deceive him and keep important secrets from him, even if it is for his own good.

At the book's opening, Harry uses magic to protect his cousin, Dudley, from the Dementors. Frightened by the Dementors' intrusion into the Muggle word and concerned that he has once again used magic outside of Hogwarts, Harry flees to London to the home of his godfather, Sirius Black. That home is also headquarters to the Order of the Phoenix, a group of wizards who have secretly banded together to fight Lord Voldemort because the corrupt Ministry of Magic refuses to acknowledge his return.

Back at Hogwarts, Harry learns that the Ministry of Magic has sent Dolores Umbridge to be the new Defense Against the Dark Arts teacher—and to monitor who agrees with or disagrees with the Ministry's point of view. Harry works hard at his studies, preparing for the O.W.L.s—Ordinary Wizarding Level exams. (These are similar to O-level, or Ordinary-Level, tests that were once given in British secondary schools.) This is made harder by the fact that Umbridge will not teach the students any actual skills needed in Defense Against the Dark Arts. To practice these skills, Harry and his friends form a secret Defense Against the Dark Arts club. But the group is caught and disbanded by Umbridge. As a result, Dumbledore resigns, and Umbridge replaces him as head of the school. After Harry finds out that Sirius is being held at the Ministry of Magic, Harry and Hermione persuade Umbridge to follow them into the forest. In the forest, centaurs help them by holding

Potter's World Becomes Even Darker

Umbridge captive, while the students use flying horses to travel to the Ministry of Magic.

At the Ministry, Harry sees a glass sphere with his and Voldemort's names on it. He is surrounded by Death Eaters who demand to know about any prophecies contained in the sphere. Harry, Ron, Hermione, Ginny, and fellow students Luna Lovegood and Neville Longbottom fight off the Death Eaters by themselves until they are joined by members of the Order of the Phoenix. It is too late. Sirius is killed by a Death Eater, and Voldemort escapes.

J. K. Rowling signs copies of *Harry Potter and the Order of the Phoenix* in a bookstore in Edinburgh, Scotland.

Heartbroken over Sirius's death, Harry learns that the prophecy in the glass sphere says that he has a power Voldemort does not know about—the power of love. The prophecy also says Harry must destroy Voldemort or be destroyed by him.

Of all the Harry Potter Books, *The Order of the Phoenix* has been said to have the highest emotional impact for its readers, probably because Harry loses his godfather. Dealing with death and bereavement are important themes in all of Rowling's books—from the murder of Harry's parents to the ultimate showdown between Harry and Voldemort.

"It's a strong central theme—dealing with death, . . . and facing up to death," said Rowling.[5]

Rowling has said there is some value to exposing children to the idea of death before they have an actual experience of it. Even so, she says she walked into the kitchen and cried after writing the death of Sirius, but she knew she had to kill off the character.[6]

While it may seem cruel that Harry loses Sirius so quickly after he has found him, death is a very real part of life, says Rowling, and to deny it makes life less real.

Every confrontation seems to help Harry grow in self-confidence. At the beginning of *The Order of the Phoenix*, Harry already has acquired enough self-confidence to stop Dudley from bullying him and to protect Dudley from the Dementors. With the help of Dumbledore, Harry has come to believe in his dreams. He has learned to trust his instincts. When Umbridge won't teach the students Defense Against the Dark Arts, he defies her and trains students for their battle with the Death Eaters.

Reading about Harry's struggles to survive and become stronger may help some readers gain the confidence needed to fight their own battles or get the

Dealing with death and bereavement are important themes in all of Rowling's books.

respect they seek. Identifying with a hero—whether the hero is found in a Greek myth, a comic book, or a Harry Potter book—may be just what it takes for a person to find the self-confidence he or she needs to succeed.[7]

Harry Potter and the Half-Blood Prince

With *Harry Potter and the Half-Blood Prince*, the series takes on a very somber mood. Lord Voldemort has returned and has assembled the Death Eaters around him. Newspapers in the wizarding world have taken to calling Harry "The Chosen One," since he alone is said to be able to defeat Lord Voldemort. Harry waits at home with the Dursleys, still mourning the death of Sirius. Dumbledore arrives to take Harry back to Hogwarts. On the way, he takes Harry to meet a former professor from Hogwarts in an effort to persuade him to return to a teaching post. The professor, Slughorn, is reluctant, but they persuade him to return as Potions teacher. Harry finds a Potions textbook with writing in it that offers hints to make potions work; it also tells how to perform spells that venture into dark magic. The book was owned by someone who called himself the Half-Blood Prince.

Professor Slughorn likes to talk about all the successful students he has had in the past, one of whom was Tom Riddle, the student who became Lord Voldemort. In order to learn more about Voldemort, Harry must convince Slughorn to share a memory he has tried to erase. Using a potion, he gets Slughorn to tell him how Voldemort learned to create Horcruxes—six containers into which the Dark Lord has divided the magical essence of himself that can be used by his followers to recreate him. If the six containers are destroyed, then Voldemort will die for good. Two have already been destroyed—Tom Riddle's diary and a ring. Two others are a locket and a Hufflepuff's cup.

Together, Harry and Dumbledore travel to a secret place visited by Voldemort, where they find a locket, one of Voldemort's Horcruxes. When they return to the school, they see the Dark Mark hovering over it. Dumbledore tells Harry to wake Snape. As Harry hurries off, he is frozen by a spell. Malfoy, Snape, and some Death Eaters arrive, and Snape kills Dumbledore. As soon as Dumbledore dies, Harry is no longer frozen. He begins to battle the Death Eaters with his friends and the Hogwarts teachers. They are driven away, but Malfoy and Snape escape.

Everyone is stunned to discover that Dumbledore has died. Harry opens the locket that they worked so hard to get and discovers it is not a Horcrux. Inside is a note that says the real container was stolen by someone with the initials R.A.B.

At the end of the book, there is no longer anyone to protect Harry—not his parents, not Sirius Black, not Dumbledore. He must go back to the Dursleys' briefly, and then he must fight Voldemort to the death.

Harry Potter and the Half-Blood Prince has been compared by reviewers to *The Lord of the Rings* because both have similar feelings of approaching doom. In some ways, the mood of *Harry Potter and the Half-Blood Prince* seems to reflect the tensions of Britain in 2005 or the mood of Europe at the dawn of World War II.

Of all the books, this is by far the most frightening. By its final pages, Harry is no longer a boy wizard but a young man. In the seventh book, he will have to defeat Voldemort or die trying. To accomplish what he has to do, he must leave his childhood behind forever.

The power of love and the importance of making the right decisions are themes reinforced in the sixth book. *Harry Potter and the Half-Blood Prince* also explores the relationships young male characters have with their fathers or father figures—Voldemort and his absent father; Draco Malfoy and his father, Lucius; Harry and his mentor Dumbledore.[8]

Rowling has said that as she looks back through the books, there is a "litany of bad fathers. That's where evil seems to flourish, in places where people didn't get good fathering."[9]

In this book, Rowling again explores the themes of death and loss. But the book's dark mood and loss of a major, much-beloved character left some young readers so grief stricken that a few critics wondered if she had abandoned her younger readers with this book.

"It's not a kid's book anymore. It's much too scary," said Nina Blass of Arlington, Massachusetts. The four-teen-year-old does not want her eight-year-old sister to read it by herself.[10]

Harry is completely on his own at the end of the book, and this leaves some young readers feeling vulnerable. "It really is frightening," said Emma Frank, a seventeen-year-old camp counselor-in-training in Brookline, Massachusetts. "But that can be a lovely and hopeful message, too: that you have to take responsibility for yourself sooner or later."[11]

There is nothing to be feared in death or darkness, Dumbledore tells Harry during a quest for the magical container. What people really fear is the unknown. The end of this book is dark with uncertainty. The book has been described as a "powerful, unforgettable setup for the finale."[12]

Harry Potter and the Deathly Hallows

As the final book begins, Harry is about to turn seventeen and must leave the Dursley home. Voldemort has gathered his dark forces and now pursues Harry openly. Harry's escape from the Dursley home results in the death of his owl, Hedwig, and the murder of Mad-Eye Moody, a member of the Order of the Phoenix who is trying to help Harry get away. Harry's scar burns more intensely as his link with Voldemort seems to grow stronger. He can sometimes see what the Dark Lord sees.

After Harry learns some disturbing information about Dumbledore's early years, he, Ron, and Hermoine receive gifts from Dumbledore's will, which include the Snitch Harry caught in his first Quidditch match. Although Dumbledore also left Harry Godric Gryffindor's sword, the Ministry keeps it.

During the wedding of Bill Weasley and Fleur Delacour, the wizarding community learns that the Ministry of Magic has fallen and Death Eaters are on their way. Harry, Ron and Hermione hide in Sirius Black's house, where they discover the whereabouts of one Horcrux, a locket, that they must destroy. When they enter the Ministry of Magic to get the Horcrux, they learn that Muggle-born wizards now must register with the Ministry to see if they have stolen the magic they command. Snape is now headmaster at Hogwarts.

Harry wants to get Godric Gryffindor's sword because it can destroy the Horcrux they have. Ron decides Harry has no definite plan and disappears. Harry and Hermione travel to Godric's Hollow, where Harry's parents are buried. There, Voldemort and his snake attack them. They escape, but Harry's wand is broken, leaving him vulnerable. While hiding in the woods, Harry sees a doe Patronus that leads him to the Gryffindor sword. Ron reappears and helps Harry free it, then uses it to break the Horcrux.

They visit Luna Lovegood's father, Xenophilius, to ask about a symbol he wears. He tells them about the

Deathly Hallows, three objects that can be used to conquer death. They include an Elder Wand, a Resurrection Stone, and a Cloak of Invisibility, which could be the cloak Harry already has. Xenophilius betrays them to the Death Eaters, but they escape.

The three friends are caught in the woods and taken to Malfoy Manor, where the Death Eaters have gathered and imprisoned Luna and Mr. Ollivander, the wandmaker. Dobby arrives to rescue them. Harry captures Draco's wand, but Dobby is killed. With the help of a goblin, the three friends then break into a vault at Gringotts, the wizarding bank. There they find another Horcrux, the Hufflepuff's cup. They escape by dragon and lose the sword to their goblin accomplice. When Voldemort learns they have the cup, he realizes they seek the Horcruxes.

Harry suspects the next Horcrux is hidden at Hogwarts. In his efforts to find and destroy it, Harry rescues Draco Malfoy from a fiery death. A battle rages at Hogwarts between the Dark Lord's forces and those who oppose him. During the battle, Harry sneaks into Voldemort's hiding place and overhears him talking to Snape. The Dark Lord decides he cannot master the Elder Wand because it belongs to Snape, so he kills him. As Snape dies, he asks Harry to capture and listen to his memories. Snape, Harry learns, had always loved Harry's mother, Lily, and was working with Dumbledore to protect Harry. Harry now realizes he must die to vanquish Voldemort.

74

Harry can now open the Snitch. Inside is the Resurrection Stone, which he uses to meet the spirits of his father, his mother, and Sirius. These spirits accompany him on what could be his final journey. Harry goes to Voldemort and surrenders to him, offering no resistance. Voldemort attacks him.

Harry awakens in a misty place, unsure if he is dead. There he meets Albus Dumbledore, who explains that Harry himself is the last Horcrux. When Voldemort attacked Harry, he destroyed that Horcrux. However, Voldemort's life also protects Harry. This happened when Voldemort took his blood at the end of *Goblet of Fire*. Because of this, Voldemort cannot kill Harry.

The wand that Voldemort uses is Dumbledore's Elder Wand, and Harry is its true master. Harry awakens, but he pretends to be dead. Voldemort marches on, forcing Hagrid to carry Harry's body. Neville kills Voldemort's snake, destroying the last Horcrux. Voldemort attacks Harry, but his wand kills Voldemort.

The book ends with an epilogue that takes place nineteen years later at platform nine and three quarters, when two of Harry and Ginny's children depart for Hogwarts. The new magical world they live in is a good one, and all is well.

A Coming-of-Age Tale

The seven-book Harry Potter series has been called a coming-of-age tale. In *Harry Potter and the Deathly Hallows*, Harry reaches the wizarding world's official age of adulthood—seventeen—and must meet adult challenges. Because he has lost all of his protectors—his parents, his godfather, Dumbledore, and even the Dursleys—he must now face the world with little guidance. He can legally practice magic, but that does not make it easier to deal with his inner doubts, his fears, and even the prospect of losing his life.

One of the lessons Harry learns in this book is the importance of trusting his own instincts, because he must often make decisions for which it seems there are no clear-cut reasons. This may be even harder for Harry than most young adults, because he grew up with relatives who did not value him or his abilities. After living in a home where he could not trust his guardians, he has to learn how to make life-long friends and trust others. He learns that friends working together can be much stronger and more effective than a single individual. Kindness shown to others throughout the series is repaid in *Harry Potter and the Deathly Hallows*, and he learns that no good deed is ever really wasted.

Harry also discovers how complicated people can be. While there is definitely good and evil in the world, good people, such as Dumbledore, can have a dark side, and seemingly evil people, such as Snape, can be brave and work for good. That last lesson is a significant part of becoming an adult. It is important to understand how complicated people can be and how easy it is to be corrupted by power. The last book is also about fighting tyranny. It shows how easy it can be to be seduced by evil. Harry learns that it is important to resist evil even when it means risking his life. He must overcome his fears to make one final sacrifice.[13]

The last book is a more adult novel than the previous six. For instance, its description of the Mudblood vs. pureblood controversy echoes the Nazi agenda during World War II, and it has scenes of torture that are horrifying, even though they are not explicit. Yet, as dark as the book often is, there is a positive, optimistic message of love, forgiveness, and the importance of showing remorse. The book is less about the power of magic, which is seen to be limited, than it is about the power of love. It proves that even magic cannot conquer death, but love can. Love has the power to create families and communities and redeem lives.

A good example of the life redeemed is that of Snape, who was seen in the previous six books as a very unlikable character. In *Harry Potter and the Deathly Hallows*, readers discover that he is a very brave person, who lived for and died for love.[14]

A generation of children have grown up with Harry Potter and faced many of the same ordinary, nonmagical challenges in school—bullying, difficult teachers, and dangerous temptations—without any magic spells to call on. Some Harry Potter fans who read the first book in elementary school were college students or working at their first job when they read the final installment. Thus, they find it easy to identify with him.

"At 15 his experiences were very similar to my experiences in a weird way," said Sarah Harper, a

77

student at Centenary College in Louisiana. "Except I wasn't fighting evil wizards at the time."[15]

As Rowling's books became more complex and the subject matter became more adult, Harry's fans kept reading, perhaps learning some of the same life lessons.

"Harry is part of a shared cultural heritage," said Philip Nel, an associate professor of English at Kansas State University. Nel teaches a course on Harry Potter and wrote *J. K. Rowling's Novels: A Reader's Guide*. "It serves as a touchstone for their experience that they can look back on and binds them as a group culturally and generationally."[16]

Harry's story, from the time he first has to endure living with his Muggle guardians to the time he sends his own children off to Hogwarts, has become a tale that has shaped—and perhaps inspired—a generation.

"This is definitely the mythical tale of our generation," said Sudipta Bandyopadhya, a Yale student who grew up reading the series. "Without a doubt, this takes place alongside the original *Star Wars* and *Lord of the Rings*."[17]

(Shortly after the publication of *Deathly Hallows*, J. K. Rowling announced—in response to a fan's question about whether Dumbledore had ever been in love—that Dumbledore was gay. Though remarked upon in the media, the announcement seemed to have little impact on the book's young fans, and it did not arouse immediate protests from conservative groups.)

Chapter 7

Challenging Harry Potter

It is a good thing Harry Potter excels at Hogwarts Academy, since J. K. Rowling's hero has faced expulsion at several schools around the United States and has even seen the welcome mat rolled up at some of the nation's public libraries.

Altogether, the Harry Potter books made the American Library Association (ALA) list of most challenged books for five consecutive years. The Potter books were the most frequently challenged books in 1999, when *Harry Potter and the Sorcerer's Stone* faced 472 challenges. In 2000, the ALA reported 646 challenges.[1]

These challenges—usually by concerned parents— were expressed in several ways. Parents sought to have the books removed from the school library. They also sought to have the books placed in a part of the library where children would need a permission slip to get them. They asked that the books not be read aloud. They asked that the books not be part of the curriculum in elementary school.

When such challenges were not successful, some parents transferred their children into other classes where the books were not being read or transferred their children to another school.

In some schools, officials honored the challenges and restricted access to the books. When some schools placed restrictions, it prompted other parents to sue for access.

Altogether, J. K. Rowling's books created quite a bit of controversy.

Challenging a Book in School

To challenge a book, parents usually write a request asking that an offending book be removed from a school curriculum or library. They must explain why they think it is inappropriate. That challenge is then usually reviewed by a school board of elected officials and then adopted or rejected as a school policy. Sometimes a committee is created to review the book by reading it or listening to testimony from parents and experts. The committee members present their opinions to the school board and officials, who make a decision.

Parents can ask that a book be banned outright or request that access be denied to children of a certain age or that to access the book at all, all children must bring written permission from their parents.

Asking that children have written permission to access the book may seem like a reasonable request, but parents who do not have any problem with the

80

challenged material say that this makes it harder for their children to be allowed to read whatever they want.

The protests against J. K. Rowling's books fall into several categories. Most parents who challenged the books were protesting what they saw as the glorification of wizards and witchcraft, which they considered evil and against Christian teachings.

The books were seen as promoting Wicca, a nature-based religion associated with some aspects of witchcraft. A few challenges were inspired by statements from religious leaders who urged parents to take a stand against what they saw as a dangerous trend.

One interdenominational Christian public policy organization that spoke out against the books was the Traditional Values Coalition (TVC). Based in Washington, D.C., TVC has stated that the Potter books are associated with the practice of Wicca, which they say "incorporates radical feminism and homosexuality into their practices." According to the coalition, Wicca also supposedly advocates abortion. The coalition admits that J. K. Rowling's books do not advocate homosexuality or abortion, but that a "child who is seduced into a Wicca through Harry Potter's books will eventually be introduced to these other concepts."[2]

Hearing members of a religious community say that reading a book can harm a child can prompt parents to take action. In January 2000, born-again Christian parents Greg and Arlena Wilson voiced such concerns to officials at Three Rivers Elementary School

A young reader devours the latest Harry Potter. Despite the books' popularity, some people are worried about the impact the books have on children.

in Bend, Oregon, upon hearing that their child, a fourth grader, might be exposed to Harry Potter.

To protect their child, they wanted the books banned in the whole school. According to the Wilsons, the fun facade of the Harry Potter books hides an immoral plot designed to foster hatred and rebellion and to promote witchcraft.

In their January 2000 complaint, they cited several disturbing examples of witchcraft they found in the book. For instance, Arlena Wilson said, "It's the fact that the evil wizard inhabits another man's body, and in order for him to stay at half power, he has to drink the blood of a unicorn."[3]

After the Wilsons made their request, the school's interim superintendent, Gary Bruner, expressed his concern that withdrawing the book would affect all children in the school system, not just their child. After listening to speakers discuss both sides of the issue, the school board voted unanimously to retain the books and keep them available without restrictions for both students and teachers.[4]

Does Potter Promote Wicca?

Reading books on wizardry in schools, some parents have complained, is the same as promoting Wicca, the religion they say is associated with witchcraft. If the schools are promoting Wicca by reading Harry Potter, say the parents lodging the complaint, then those schools violate the First Amendment to the

Constitution, which demands the separation of church and state.

The framers of the Constitution wrote rules about the separation of church and state into the Constitution because they wanted to avoid the religious wars that had torn apart so many European nations. The First Amendment begins with these words: "Congress shall make no law respecting an establishment of religion, or prohibiting the free exercise thereof." This means that neither the state nor the federal government can set up a church or make laws that prefer one religion over the other. The government cannot endorse or promote a religion or any religious principles—be they Christian, Jewish, Muslim, or Wiccan.

How the First Amendment applies to events and shapes school rules is often up for debate. Is it okay to display a representation of the infant Jesus in the manger at Christmastime? Or sing Christmas carols? Should there be a menorah for Hanukkah and a Christmas tree? Can Muslim girls wear head scarves in school when no one else is allowed to wear a hat? These are just a few examples of the kinds of controversies that have arisen over religious expression in public schools.

Most Wiccans say that the Harry Potter books have nothing to do with Wicca, noting that the religion is based in nature and has nothing to do with witchcraft and certainly nothing to do with black magic. Peter Mather, a Wiccan priest in Plymouth, New Hampshire, read the books to see if they had anything to do with his religion. He wanted to see what was in them before he let his children read them.

"I must say that these books no more promote witchcraft than *Anne of Green Gables* promotes moving to Nova Scotia," said Mather.[5]

In York, Pennsylvania, some taxpayers disagreed. A concerned mother, Deb DiEugenio, and a pastor, Tony Leanza, asked the Eastern York District to ban the

> *"I must say that these books no more promote witchcraft than* Anne of Green Gables *promotes moving to Nova Scotia."*

Potter series on the principle of separation of church and state. DiEugenio said she did not want to pay taxes to teach her daughter witchcraft.

The Reverend Tony Leanza of the New Wine Christian Center argued that since Wicca was a religion, the books has no place in schools. The school board disagreed. They voted 7 to 2 to continue to use the series. Any student who received a parent's permission could participate.[6]

Promoting bad behavior is another reason some parents give for disliking the books. They say that having Harry as a hero could encourage children to break rules. In the Potter books, Harry and his friends often seem to take rules lightly, wandering around the halls after curfew, leaving school when they are not supposed to, practicing magic when they are forbidden to, and organizing a Defense Against the Dark Arts class when their teacher won't instruct them in these skills.

"Stealing, lies, hate, revenge, and even murder are presented in a complete absence of moral conflict," said Kenneth McCormick, a father of two in Birchrunville, Pennsylvania, in a letter to his local newspaper. "Lying exists, of course, in the plots of many children's books, but there is normally an at least tacit recognition that lying is a moral problem of some sort."[7]

Although Harry is sometimes punished, his defiance of authority usually turns out to have been a good thing. Some parents see this as a bad lesson for a child to learn.

Another criticism was that the Potter books promote the use of magical thinking—a belief that thoughts and words can cause actions—and would thereby keep children from learning to solve problems in practical ways in the real world. This type of thinking may be especially appealing to children who are troubled or whose lives are more difficult than those of their classmates and friends.

Dark themes and scary scenes were other criticisms. As Rowling has admitted, the books do get darker as the series progresses, with characters struggling with inner conflicts and dangerous enemies—and some of them even dying.

"The books have a serious tone of death, lack of respect and sheer evil," said Elizabeth Mounce of Columbia, South Carolina, who asked the state's board of education to remove the books from school libraries.[8]

The publication of the first two books may also have sparked so much controversy because of current events in 1999 and 2000. The violence in the books was protested not only because parents saw it as inappropriate for children, but because it might inspire violent actions as children became adolescents. A few parents made a connection between the reading of violent books and the actions of the two students who killed and injured fellow students and teachers in the 1999 Columbine High School shooting incident in Littleton, Colorado. The release of these books shortly around the time of that incident—and similar acts of school-related violence inspired by the original incident—contributed to parents' concerns.

"As we expose our kids to the occult, we expose our kids to blood, to violence, and desensitize them to that," said the Reverend Lori Jo Schepers of Zeeland, Michigan. "What I can expect is those kids, as they mature, have a very good chance of becoming another Dylan Klebold and those guys in Columbine."[9]

"How many more school shootings linked to students acting out these fairy tales and fantasies do we have to endure before this type of material is not read and promoted in our own school system?" asked Steve Mounce of Columbia, South Carolina, when he requested that the South Carolina Board of Education remove the books from the school library shelves.[10]

But is reading about something the same as promoting or teaching it? Does reading about Adolf Hitler promote Nazism? Would reading *The Diary of Anne Frank* encourage Nazism? Does reading about the racism rampant when Mark Twain wrote *Huckleberry*

Finn encourage racist actions? Or does reading about a wrong taking place lead a thoughtful person to want to right it? It is a question that is as old as books and one many books have been written about.

"Some people believe that just the act of reading Harry will … automatically convert readers into witches," said Judith Krug, director of the ALA's Office of Intellectual Freedom. Also, Krug said that parents who protested the books tended to see the books as glorifying evil rather than as a struggle between good and evil.[11]

Potter on Trial

A sampling of some of the challenges to J. K. Rowling's books offers insights into why the books offended people who had read them and even those who had only heard about them. These cases can also demonstrate how the right to free speech is interpreted—in challenges to the books, challenges to the restrictions placed on these books, and how these challenges were resolved. Some of these cases were dealt with within a school system, and one case was settled by the judicial system.

November 1999. When Cynthia Kersey's son, a student at Simi Elementary School in Simi Valley, California, brought home a copy of *Harry Potter and the Sorcerer's Stone* in November 1999, she was more than a little worried. The book being read aloud in her son's class seemed to promote the practice of witchcraft, a subject Kersey had heard the killers at Columbine High School were very interested in.

Kersey brought her concerns to the school, asking administrators to remove the book from the school curriculum. A committee of parents, teachers, and administrators read the book and decided to continue to allow it to be read aloud. However, kids whose parents object can now read something else.[12]

That same month, Gary Feenstra, a school superintendent in Zeeland, Michigan, read the first Harry Potter book, then placed restrictions on displaying, reading, and borrowing it. The book would not be on library shelves, students could only take it out with a signed permission slip, it could not be used in the school curriculum, and no further copies would be purchased for the schools.

Feenstra made his decision by discussing the book with other educators and reading criticisms, but he did not ask the school's board to review the issue. The school board decided not to discuss the issue, but parents attended a meeting and a few spoke up in defense of the books.[13]

"I'm here to ask that this board free Harry Potter," said Mary Van Harn of Zeeland. "I could use those books to teach Sunday School. They're filled with role models."[14]

Students created a Web site to get the schools to reinstate the books. A variety of free-speech organizations wrote to the schools, noting that the students' First Amendment rights of free access to information were being violated.

Active in this effort was a newly formed group that called itself Muggles for Harry Potter. The group consists of eight groups that promote freedom of expression as part of their involvement in the protection of First Amendment rights. They include the American Booksellers Foundation for Free Expression, the Freedom to Read Foundation, the Association of American Publishers, the National Council of Teachers of English, the Children's Book Council, the Association of Booksellers for Children, the National Coalition Against Censorship, and the PEN American Center.[15]

An advisory committee was formed and suggested that Superintendent Feenstra put the books back in the elementary and middle schools, to permit readings in middle schools, and to let children use them in book reports. He did.

Some restrictions remain, however. In the Zeeland school district, teachers may not read the Potter books aloud to elementary school students, but students can take them from the library.

November 1999. Parents also complained about the Potter books in the Frankfort School District in Frankfort, Illinois. Parents originally asked the superintendent, Pamela Witt, to ban Harry Potter books because they contain lying and "smart-aleck retorts to adults."

School officials decided not to censor the Potter books but to allow parents to remove their children from any reading sessions they consider inappropriate.

Superintendent Witt said that deciding what was appropriate reading material for each individual child was not the teacher's responsibility.

"We're not going to censor; that's the parents' responsibility," said Witt.[16]

In January 2000, another school official, Joan Bookman, principal at the Carrollwood Elementary School in Tampa, Florida, banned the ordering of more Potter books for the school library, even though there were no complaints from parents. The one library copy could remain there and students could bring the book to school.[17]

It was because of the witchcraft themes, said the principal. "We just knew that we had some parents who wouldn't want their children to read these books."[18]

March 2000. In Cedar Rapids, Iowa, parents Brad and Brenda Birdnow asked that *Harry Potter and the Sorcerer's* Stone be removed from school libraries. They objected to the romantic characterization of witches and warlocks, which they said could erode the morality of children and therefore, ultimately, society.[19]

A committee of parents, teachers, and students decided that no restrictions should be placed on the books. Their consensus was that the book was enjoyable and well-written and that the magic in it was used in the context of a fantasy story. It was a story in which good triumphed over evil, and the committee felt it did not try to convert anyone to satanism.

April 2000. Fifty-three parents at the Orange Grove Elementary School in Whittier, California, requested that all Potter books be banned at the school. The parents said that the series not only promoted black magic but also subjected young readers to bad experiences.

A district committee rejected their request and said that if all books were banned from school due to violence, "Hansel and Gretel," "Little Red Riding Hood" and the "Three Little Pigs" would have to go as well.[20]

September 2000. In Dallas, Texas, parents challenged *Harry Potter and the Sorcerer's Stone,* complaining that the book promoted violence and deception. Reading it might give children the wrong message, they said.

The district surveyed teachers, who were overwhelmingly in favor of unrestricted access to the books. The school board voted 3 to 1 in favor of that decision.

One of the challenging parents, Michelle Cox, was not pleased with the ruling. She said the board seemed more concerned about what teachers thought than what parents were concerned about.[21]

October 2000. Janet Weaver asked the Arab, Alabama, Board of Education to remove the Harry Potter books from her child's school library and curriculum. Rowling was a member of the occult, said Weaver, and reading her books encourages children to practice witchcraft. "We need to put God back in the schools and throw the Harry Potter books out," said Weaver.

When Weaver complained, school superintendent Edwin Cooley explained to her that there were no Harry Potter books at Arab Primary school, which her child attended, and only two or three at other elementary, junior high, and high schools in the district. Most of the books read in school were purchased by parents.

"You don't want to start banning books like the Harry Potter books because you don't know where it will lead," said Cooley.

Three review committees recommended keeping the books, but it was decided that the school district's teachers could not assign them as required reading.[22]

November 2000. Rather than ban the books outright, some schools have responded to parental concern by requiring children to bring in a permission slip from their parents if they want to read certain books.

That is what happened in Santa Fe, Texas. Because of calls about the subject matter, the Santa Fe Independent School District now requires written permission before students can check out any of the Harry Potter novels. This policy limits access to the books that some parents in this largely Southern Baptist community might not find acceptable. At the time of the ruling, the J. K. Rowling novels were the only books singled out.[23]

November 2000. In Bristol, New Hampshire, Julie Barker, the mother of three children in the Newfound Area School District, asked the school to ban classroom readings of the books because they taught witchcraft and wizardry and dark, scary themes.

However, the school's principal, George Kelley, stated that the books don't teach witchcraft or wizardry. "These books are fiction," said Kelley.

In this case, the school board voted against a proposal that parents be informed ahead of books being read in class so they could approve or disapprove of the curriculum. The board noted that parents always have the right to request an alternative assignment.[24]

In the 2001-2002 school year, Potter books were challenged in twenty-one school districts.[25]

July 2002. One elementary school that voted to restrict access to the Potter books had that decision challenged by one of its students and her family. Restricting that student's access to the Harry Potter books was ruled unconstitutional in court.

In Cedarville, Arkansas, parents asked that J. K. Rowling's books be taken out of general circulation because they dealt with the occult and promoted disobedience and disrespect—portraying authority as "stupid" and magic as "good." The school board voted to place the books in a special section of the library and require students to get a signed permission slip from their parents before they could borrow the books.

A fourth-grade student, Dakota Counts, and her parents, Billy Ray Counts and Mary Nell Counts, were upset by this ruling and sued the school to lift the restrictions.[26] Children's author Judy Blume and several free-speech organizations helped the Counts family file their case.[27]

Attorney Brian Meadors, representing the Counts family, noted that three of the school board members who voted for restricting the books had strong views against witchcraft and were using the school board to impose their own religious views.

The district court overturned the board's decision and ordered the books to be returned to regular shelves in the library. The court ruled that denying students access to the books was in violation of their First Amendment rights. The court ruled that even though the schools were trying to protect students, they were still bound by the Bill of Rights, and regardless of their personal feelings, school board members did not have the power to restrict others' access to the books.[28]

August 2002. "Witchcraft is of the devil and the devil is very powerful," said Ron Rio, a West Hartford, Connecticut, resident at a board of education meeting that reminded some of those present of what they had heard about the Salem witchcraft trials.

Rio was one of a group of people calling for a school system-wide ban on all materials dealing with witchcraft and witches, including the Harry Potter series. The group also protested school trips to Salem, Massachusetts. The school board did not take any action on the group's petition requesting a curriculum review, since it was not an official form.

"If we took all the books off the school shelves that people had a problem with, we wouldn't have any books," said another parent, Eileen Branciforte.[29]

August 2005. Laura Mallory asked that the Harry Potter books be removed from the classrooms and libraries of her children's schools in Loganville, Georgia, because, she said, they promoted the dangerous practices of Wicca.

The attorney representing the Cedarville parents poses with *Harry Potter and the Sorcerer's Stone.* Opponents asked that the Rowling books be removed from general circulation in the school libraries.

"With the deceptive, exciting, children-friendly packaging of witchcraft in the Harry Potter series, our youth today view witchcraft not only as good and fun, but also as harmless fantasy," said Mallory on her Web site.[30]

When the Georgia State Board of Education decided to retain the books on December 14, 2006, Mallory filed a request for an appeal to the Superior Court of Gwinnett County. In May 2007, a Gwinnett Superior Court judge ruled that the books could remain on school bookshelves. Mallory acknowledges that she has not actually read the books.[31]

Private Schools and Harry Potter

Private schools can restrict reading material in any way they deem appropriate and do not have to satisfy First Amendment rights. In 2000, the Holy Family Catholic School of Rockford, Illinois, removed Rowling's books from the library because of their positive portrayal of witchcraft and fortune-telling, both of which are contrary to Church teachings. Several religious schools have banned the books.[32]

After one English school banned the Potter books, a head teacher there compared the danger of letting children read them to the danger of exposing children to a pedophile. The books were banished from the library at St. Mary's Island Church of England Aided School, where the head teacher said that "devils, demons, and witches are real and pose the same threat as, say, a child molester."[33]

97

The controversy over Harry Potter has even reached the Vatican. When asked about the books, Pope John Paul II said the stories helped children see the difference between good and evil. A Vatican spokesman, Father Peter Fleetwood, said British author J. K. Rowling was "Christian by conviction, is Christian in her mode of living, even in her way of writing."[34]

However, Cardinal Joseph Ratzinger, who succeeded John Paul II to become Pope Benedict XVI in 2005, had a different point of view, which he had already expressed before becoming pope. In an earlier interview, he had said the books "erode Christianity in the soul" of young people and are inconsistent with the teachings of the Catholic Church.

"If we took all the books off the school shelves that people had a problem with, we wouldn't have any books."

He made this statement to Gabriele Kuby in March 2003 in an interview for Kuby's book, *Harry Potter: Good or Evil?* In her book, Ratzinger described the books as a "subtle seduction."[35]

This opinion is expected to affect the way Catholic schools choose to use or reject the books.

Student Withdrawals

Being unable to remove the Potter books from the curriculum has made some parents so angry that they have moved their child from one class to another and even from one school to another.

98

For example, in November 1999, in Moorpark, California, Dominic and Teresa Schmidt removed their child from his fourth-grade class because they didn't want him reading books that talked about death and killing and drinking animal blood.

"This is witchcraft, and as a religion, it doesn't belong in school," said Teresa Schmidt.

She asked that the books be banned in the whole school district and said Potter's popularity was not a good argument for keeping him. Tongue piercing and crack are popular too, she said.

She transferred her child to another school after a principal-ordered review recommended that the school district keep the books and the school's Parent Teacher Association endorsed the books.[36]

Public Libraries and Events

Challenges to Pottermania have not been limited to schools. There have also been challenges to Potter-related programs at public libraries and public events.

In Oskaloosa, Kansas, a "Muggle Studies" for "aspiring young witches and wizards" program at a library was canceled because of parent protests. Parents expressed fear that their children would be taught witchcraft at the event.[37]

A parent threatened the Jacksonville, Florida, Public Library with a lawsuit for passing out a Hogwarts Certificate of Accomplishment to children who read all of *Harry Potter and the Goblet of Fire*. The parent, John Miesburg, said that witchcraft was a religion and the mock diplomas violated the separation of church and state. The library ceased its promotion.[38]

Police in Penryn, Pennsylvania, refused to volunteer to direct traffic for a Young Men's Christian Association (YMCA) triathlon because Harry Potter was read to kids attending the YMCA after-school program.

The Penryn fire and police departments voted to boycott the triathlon because the YMCA was not doing "the will of God." The triathlon proceeded as planned with no traffic accidents, and the YMCA program continued to read the books.[39]

Pronouncements and Book Burnings

Book burnings and shreddings have followed strong statements delivered from the pulpit. In December 2001, evangelist Pat Robertson warned that God will forsake nations that tolerate witchcraft. Of the Harry Potter books and TV shows and films that focus on witchcraft, he said, "Now we're welcoming this and teaching our children. And what we're doing is asking for the wrath of God to come on this country."[40]

That same month, Christ Community Church in Alamogordo, New Mexico, staged a Harry Potter bonfire into which they threw J. K. Rowling's books and works by Shakespeare and J.R.R. Tolkien as well as *Cosmo Girl* and *Young Miss* magazines and other "masterpieces of Satanic deception." [41]

The event drew several hundred congregants and as many as eight hundred counterprotesters.[42]

Challenging Harry Potter

Other book burnings followed in March 2001, when J. K. Rowling's books were torched by the Harvest Assembly of God Church in Penn Town, Pennsylvania, and by the Jesus Non-Denominational Church in Greenville, Michigan.[43]

Members of the Jesus Party in Lewiston, Maine, also wanted to burn the books but had to settle for shredding them, since they could not get a permit for the bonfire.[44]

"Reading a Harry Potter book is gonna make you dirty," said the Reverend Douglas Taylor at the book shredding. He hoped to protect young readers from the books because, he said, they deal with paganism.[45]

In Maine, some opponents of the Harry Potter books resorted to cutting them up when they could not get a permit to burn them.

While burning or shredding books may seem more dramatic, banning books is more threatening to those who feel it infringes on their First Amendment rights.

The attempts to ban Harry Potter in schools have raised some important questions: Do parents have a right to protect their children from what they consider immoral or inappropriate reading material? If so, how far does that right extend? Who decides what is right to read? Can one person or one group of people decide what is right for everyone? Can't a school set a moral standard?

The U.S. Constitution—and its Bill of Rights—is always being revised and reinterpreted as views on what is right or wrong change. Once the Bill of Rights was interpreted to mean that slavery was constitutional, then it was decided that it was not. While voting was always considered a basic citizen's right, it was less than a century ago that women gained the right to vote. The Eighteenth Amendment made alcohol illegal in 1920, but in 1933 it was repealed.

According to the First Amendment Center, freedom of religion, speech, press, assembly, and petition are fundamental rights that every American is entitled to. How these rights are interpreted in the future and how that affects books such as Rowling's remains to be seen.

Chapter 8

Does Harry Potter Matter?

Some people ask: Can a boy who gets boys to read really be evil? The fact that the Harry Potter series has made children eager to read makes it a hit with many parents, teachers, and especially librarians. Tamara Stewart, a young adult librarian at the public library in Ossining, New York, was hired in 2004 because the young adult programs needed a push.

"It was definitely a struggle to get teens to come to the library. At that age, the library is not a cool place," said Stewart. "So we tried to figure out how to get more teens to take part."

Inspired by the publication of the sixth Harry Potter book, Stewart organized a three-week program for children and teens that included showing the first three movies, an astrology workshop, Potter games, and several crafts sessions, which used a Sorting Hat to sort participants into groups.

The program did really well. On opening day, despite torrential rains and flooding, eighty-one young people showed up. "We got regulars and some children that don't normally come to the library," said Stewart.

She was concerned that the astrology workshop she planned would raise some eyebrows because it could be linked to the occult, but she received no complaints. "I had parents come up to me and say that it was so great that I was doing these programs."

It is easy for Stewart to see why Rowling resonates with young and old readers alike. She said:

> Rowling is masterful at creating something that stands by itself, is original and yet familiar, with all kinds of mythic threads running through it. She really did her homework. The readers who started the series as kids are teens now. It's all about growing up and, let's face it, you are either about to go through it, you are going through it or you have gone through it. It's something that everyone can relate to.

Stewart has also seen children work on their reading skills just to be able to take part in the trend.

"They really challenge themselves to improve their reading skills," said Stewart. She dressed up as Madame Tamara, a la Professor Trelawney (a Hogwarts teacher of divination), to run the astrology workshop.[1]

Turning Boys into Readers

Debbie Williams, a children's book buyer in England, found that while the series had a strong influence on literacy for all young readers, the effect on boys was even

104

more noticeable. It encouraged boys to read more, especially boys ages nine to fourteen—traditionally not a group that was interested in reading books.

"Reading books is now cool and has a playground credibility," said Williams.[2]

Not only did the books turn children into readers—and rereaders—of this particular series, but they also made children become interested in similar books by other authors. While waiting for the next installment of the Harry Potter series, children explored other science fiction and fantasy books, like those written by C. S. Lewis, Ursula LeGuin, Diana Wynne Jones, and Madeleine L'Engle. Libraries have even launched "what to read while you're waiting for the next Harry Potter" reading campaigns. For librarians like Tamara Stewart, getting kids to read more—especially teens—can only be a good thing.

Rowling Is Surprised

It was quite a surprise to J. K. Rowling that anyone would find her books objectionable.

"Occasionally, I wonder, have they read the books? I think they're very moral books. If we're going to object to depicting magic in books, then we are going to have to reject C. S. Lewis. We're going to have to get rid of the Wizard of Oz," said Rowling.[3]

Rowling denies that she has ever used magic to promote the occult. "I think that's utter garbage. I absolutely do not believe in the occult, practice the occult.... I've met literally thousands of children now.

Not one of them has said to me, you've really turned me on to the occult, not one of them."[4]

Using tales of magic and wizards to teach children about good and evil is a time-honored tradition. "You find magic, witchcraft and all those things throughout children's literature," said Rowling.[5]

Wizards and Magic Worlds

Author Judy Blume, herself a regular on the banned children's book lists, was not surprised when she heard that Rowling had joined the ranks.

"If children are excited about a book, it must be suspect," said Blume.

When Blume and her husband were children, they read straight through L. Frank Baum's Oz series and learned all about wizards and flying witches. Reading about flying witches taught her imagination to soar, she said, but the most important lesson she learned from those books was that she loved to read.[6]

It wasn't only authors whose books had been banned who defended Rowling. At a time when the Harry Potter books received a lot of criticism from conservative, mostly Christian groups, Christian author Connie Neal came out in their defense. Neal saw them as being similar to other children's classics and also containing valuable character lessons.

"Most parents allow their children to entertain some 'magic' in fantasy stories and trust it will be understood within that context," says Neal, author of

106

What's a Christian to Do With Harry Potter? and *The Gospel According to Harry Potter*.

One example of a now-acceptable magical character that she mentions is Glinda the Good Witch from the Wizard of Oz series.[7]

Baum's stories about a girl named Dorothy who lands in the magical kingdom of Oz have been challenged repeatedly. An assembly of librarians once objected to the books because they were "unwholesome" and "not serious literature."[8]

Also, some critics had a problem with the favorable portrayal of Glinda the Good Witch, whose kind nature they thought might promote an interest in witchcraft. The Oz books are an example of books that were controversial when first released but over time came to be considered classics.

Why Does Harry Seem Familiar?

The Harry Potter books have also been compared to *The Hobbit* and *The Lord of the Rings* by J.R.R. Tolkien and even more often to the Narnia books by C. S. Lewis, which include *The Magician's Nephew, The Lion, the Witch and the Wardrobe, The Horse and His Boy, Prince Caspian, The Voyage of the Dawn Treader, The Silver Chair,* and *The Last Battle*.

In *The Lion, the Witch and the Wardrobe,* the best known of the Narnia books, four English children enter the magical kingdom of Narnia through an enchanted wardrobe. There they meet a wicked witch who has enchanted the world into a permanent state of winter.

Tamara Stewart, a librarian in New York, organized a Harry Potter program that was hugely popular with both children and teens. Stewart dressed up like Professor Trelawney to lead an astrology workshop.

Eventually they meet the world's true ruler, a lion named Aslan. Together, they engage in battling evil.

Narnia Versus Hogwarts

The Narnia stories have been suggested as a preferable alternative to the Harry Potter books because of their Christian imagery. In these books, Aslan is said to represent Christ, and evil magic—the kind that does not originate from Aslan—is doomed to be defeated. Another reason a conservative Christian audience might prefer the Narnia books is the popularity of Lewis's adult books on Christianity. Yet the Narnia books also contain mythological characters, examples of witchcraft, and astrology. The stories are often violent, featuring battles to the death.

While the books are now praised as endorsing traditional values, they have also been challenged. In the Howard County, Maryland, school system, parents complained that the books did not promote Christian beliefs and contain "graphic violence, mysticism, and gore."[9]

Like Rowling, Lewis said he never intended to write for children. He said he wrote for the childlike, whether his readers were five, fifty, or seventy-five. He also said that "a children's story which is enjoyed only by children is a bad children's story."[10]

Lewis and Tolkien were great friends. Reading Tolkien's stories, said Lewis, helped him to become a practicing Christian and inspired him to write his own children's stories. Although he died before Rowling was

109

even born, Lewis may have summed up the reason for the success of her books.

"We long to go through the looking glass, to reach fairyland," said Lewis, referring to the magic mirror in Lewis Carroll's *Through the Looking-Glass*, the sequel to *Alice in Wonderland*. "We also long to be the immensely popular and successful schoolboy or schoolgirl."[11]

Tolkien and Harry Potter

In J.R.R. Tolkien's *The Hobbit,* a hobbit named Bilbo Baggins is asked by the wizard Gandalf to go on an adventure. Most hobbits are not very daring, but Bilbo is not an ordinary hobbit. His travels bring him into contact with trolls, dwarves, and elves. Bilbo finds a powerful ring lost by a creature named Gollum. After several battles and defeating a dragon, Bilbo returns home and leaves the ring to his nephew Frodo.

The Lord of the Rings is a trilogy, a group of three books—*The Fellowship of the Ring, The Two Towers,* and *The Return of the King*—that continues the story. In the first book, Frodo is visited by Gandalf, who tells him that this ring is one of the Rings of Power. If the evil villain Sauron can get hold of the ring again, he can rule the world.

The loathsome creature that is Gollum was originally hobbit-like, but the ring enslaved him. The ring represents power and the evil it can do. Using it can make a person an evil shadow of his or her former self. After many battles that unite all the forces of good,

Sauron and the forces of evil are defeated. Frodo and his friends return home.

Tolkien, a staunch Roman Catholic, said he incorporated Christian values into his books. For some, this makes his books a preferable alternative to the Harry Potter series.

"It is in the details of that great trilogy's plot and characters that most readers sense Tolkien's Christian conviction. Here are self-sacrifice, courage, and pity, set over against greed, vainglory, and the lust for power," said Chris Armstrong in *Christianity Today*.[12]

Followers of many religions and of no religion at all have identified with the mythical quest in these books. Even though fans may see them as containing positive values, *The Lord of the Rings* trilogy has also been challenged in schools. Most recently, *The Hobbit* was challenged in 2002 in Willis, Texas, schools for "mysticism and paganism."[13]

Other Christian Views on Harry

Conservative Christian opposition to the Harry Potter books has lessened since the first book was published, because of the publication of favorable opinions by respected Christian writers, such as Connie Neal, and perhaps also because of people's exposure to the movies.

Neal started reading the books to find out if they were suitable for her children, and she was impressed by the content. As is the case in all classic fantasy stories, Neal says, Harry is born in a dismal setting, suffers from injustice, is unaware of his true heritage, is led to a magical world, feels hopeful but struggles with doubt, discovers he has special talents, grows in maturity, and battles evil. Yes, some of the books are frightening, but that is not necessarily a bad thing.

"Fears are challenging. Facing those fears and beating them are grand for the child. It makes him feel older and more mature. So stories that help kids process fear serve a useful purpose," said Neal.[14]

Just a Bad Kid?

Harry Potter has been criticized for having many character flaws—he is accused of being disrespectful, angry, defiant, and more. Yet in each of the works of Tolkien, Lewis, Baum, and Rowling, flawed characters struggle to achieve goodness and greatness. The Tin Man and the Cowardly Lion who accompany Dorothy to Oz must overcome the lack of a heart and a cowardly nature to reach their goal. Bilbo and Frodo must overcome laziness and fear to save the world.

The four children in *The Lion, the Witch, and the Wardrobe* must overcome their shortcomings to become noble—even becoming kings and queens. Edmund can be greedy. Susan is sometimes vain. Peter can be arrogant. Lucy is often timid. The lesson in these books is that you don't need to be perfect to achieve your goals; you must just work at them—and keep working at them.

Rowling has acknowledged that Harry Potter is a human boy who makes mistakes but strives to do the right thing. Harry, who has grown up in a world largely hostile to him, must learn to trust himself and others.

112

He must learn to control his emotions. His imaginative "magical" nature is what will help him realize those goals, but while growing up, he has been criticized for these very qualities.

Also, says Neal, reading the books is an accomplishment in itself—they're huge books, longer than the average adult novel. Children are willing to read that much because the books touch on emotions children really feel. The characters in the stories develop real skills and abilities that help them feel competent.[15]

Charles Colson, a *Christianity Today* columnist and head of Breakpoint Ministries, has pointed out that

"Fears are challenging. Facing those fears and beating them are grand for the child."

while Harry and his friends cast spells, read crystal balls, and turn themselves into animals, they don't really make contact with the supernatural world.

"The magic in these books is purely mechanical," Colson says.[16] Rowling merely uses the magic to frame the stories, as Shakespeare, Tolkien, and others have done.

In his columns, Colson has praised Harry and his friends for their courage, loyalty, and willingness to risk their lives for one another. Colson says parents who read the books with their children can use them to illustrate what's evil in the world and how you must fight that evil.

113

John Killinger, a Christian youth minister who wrote *God, the Devil, and Harry Potter,* describes the books as having a strong sense of faith and being all about the determined struggle against evil and darkness.[17] "With Harry Potter in his finest moments, we feel a sense of deep and quiet reverence, an obligation to all that is, and we know—we *know*—that evil cannot finally win," said Killinger.[18]

When Harry dropped off the ALA's most challenged books list in 2004, Reg Grant, a professor at Dallas Theological Seminary, had seen it coming. According to Grant, a growing number of Christians have realized that the books provide valuable lessons for children. "I think the movies illustrated how much Christian theology has in common with the message of Harry Potter," said Grant.[19]

The final book, *Harry Potter and the Deathly Hallows*, includes some Christian references and, some say, a Christian message. The inscriptions on the tomb of Harry's parents and on the tombs of Dumbledore's mother and sister are quotes from the New Testament that serve as important clues for Harry's quest. Rowling may never have meant to write about Christian principles, yet to some readers, the messages of love conquering death is just that.[20]

According to Nancy Carpentier Brown, author of *The Mystery of Harry Potter: A Catholic Family Guide*, and a former opponent of the novels:

114

Rowling has packaged a Christian story with a wrapping of witchcraft and magic, and through this disguise had drawn millions of children—millions of adults to read a redemptive moral story that perhaps can teach more than a religion class ever could.[21]

Wiccan Words

As to the claims that Rowling promotes Wicca, some followers of this pagan religion find the association offensive. In the video *Harry Potter—Witchcraft Repackaged: Making Evil Look Innocent,* filmmaker Robert McGee says the books accurately present Wicca, but many Wiccans say that associating flying broomsticks and the like with Wicca is about as accurate as associating Christians with Easter bunnies.[22]

Marysia Kolodziej, a twenty-seven-year-old in London who describes herself as a practicing witch, says there is little crossover between the world of Wicca and witchcraft.

"In this book, the only relevant topics are divination classes and a brief discussion of life after death. Magic in Harry Potter is a science, not an art, a fact, not a philosophy or religion," says Kolodziej.[23]

Are Girls Treated Fairly?

A few readers have expressed problems with Rowling's portrayal of women—at least in the early books.

While it is true that Harry's mother plays a very important role in the books, having sacrificed herself for her son, readers have wondered why most women and girls in the Potter series tend to have supporting roles and are not as well developed as the male characters.

Even though Rowling is a woman and now the mother of two daughters, her main character is a boy, and most of the action in the books is carried out by boys and men. There are more male professors than female. The headmaster is a man. The villain is a man. The Minister of Magic is a man. You read more about Ron than you do about Hermione.[24]

Hermione is smart and one of Harry's best friends, but she occasionally comes across as "a bossy know-it-all." She is also portrayed as being more emotional than Harry or Ron, at least outwardly. Although she is one of the brightest students at Hogwarts, in moments of real danger, Hermione sometimes falls apart.[25]

Rowling has acknowledged that she based Hermione on herself. She also found it odd that the main character of her story was a boy, but she saw Hermione as such an important part of the books that she did not feel guilty about giving her a secondary role.[26]

Although Hermione is not always likeable, both Ron and Harry also have their own less-than-likable qualities. Each of the three friends grows up as the books progress. As Hermione matures, she learns fairly quickly how to stop lecturing and communicate more effectively with her friends. She learns to share her knowledge and saves the day on more than one occasion.

Most young readers see her as a strong character and a girl who will grow into a strong woman.[27]

Where Did Rowling Get Her Story?

Since authors are often also enthusiastic readers, it can be hard to tell how much they are influenced by what they have read—or when they cross over the line between being influenced by something they've read and stealing an idea.

The lesson in these books is that you don't need to be perfect to achieve your goals; you must just work at them—and keep working at them.

While Rowling admits to being influenced by several authors, she has also been accused of borrowing large parts of her stories from the works of Tolkien, Egyptian mythology, C. S. Lewis, Jane Yolen, Diana Wynne Jones, and Edith Nesbitt, as well as specific books: *The Worst Witch* by Jill Murphy, Monica Furlong's *Wise Child*, Ursula LeGuin's *Earthsea*, *Groosham Grange* by Anthony Horowitz, and *Tom Brown's School Days* by C. Graham Baker.

All writers are influenced by the books they have enjoyed reading, but deliberately stealing the whole plot or main elements of a book is against the law. To steal an idea from a person is called plagiarism, and the person who had the original idea can take the person to

117

court to ask for payment for those ideas. Rowling has admitted that she enjoyed reading many of these books and was inspired to write something similar but insists that Harry Potter and his world are her own creation. She says she has never knowingly stolen anyone's ideas.

Nancy Stouffer, author of *The Legend of Rah and the Muggles* and *Larry Potter and His Best Friend Lilly,* sued Rowling because, she said, Rowling's books were based on her ideas. Stouffer lost her case in 2002 and was fined for making her claim with forged documents.[28]

No other author has made the claim that Rowling has stolen an idea.

Classic Literature or a Casual Read?

Are the Harry Potter books merely a quick, fun read or a serious addition to the world of children's literature? Only time will tell.

Not all reviewers are enchanted with Rowling's style of writing. *Harry Potter and the Half-Blood Prince* received reviews that ranged from "pedestrian" to "a classic." Anthony Holden, a columnist at the British paper *The Guardian,* is not a fan. He says that Rowling's stories are all black and white, her story lines are predictable, the suspense in her stories is minimal, and the writing is very sentimental.[29]

After reading a few pages of *Harry Potter and the Sorcerer's Stone,* Yale professor Harold Bloom said he found Rowling's prose style heavy on the clichés. On page 4 alone, he said, he counted seven clichés.

118

"One can reasonably doubt that *Harry Potter and the Sorcerer's Stone* is going to prove a classic of children's literature," said Bloom in 2000.[30]

A person might say that the hundreds of millions of Rowling's books sold since that time have proven this prediction to be false. There is no way to know how popular the books will be fifty or a hundred years from now. Perhaps only some of the books in the series will be remembered, as was the case with the first Oz book written by L. Frank Baum. Perhaps they all will.

This is one battle where the odds are in Harry's favor.

Chapter 9

Breaking the Spell: Ending the Harry Potter Series

By the time of the publication of *Harry Potter and the Deathly Hallows* in 2007, J. K. Rowling had been working on the Harry Potter books for seventeen years. A lot happened to her in that time.

Rowling had gone from being so poor that she could not afford decent child care to having acquired a fortune larger than that of the queen of England. Rowling also went from being able to sit quietly in a café without being recognized by strangers to being a household name.

In those seventeen years, Rowling created an alternate reality that millions of adults and children longed to escape to. She created characters people feel they know and terms—such as *Muggles*—that have become part of the English language. Many people did not want the series to end, but it had to.

Since J. K. Rowling spent almost twenty years thinking and writing about her favorite characters—Harry, Ron, and Hermione—it is not surprising that she felt sad after finishing the series, but she also felt very proud of her accomplishment.

"I can hardly believe that I've finally written the ending I've been planning for so many years. I've never felt such a mixture of extreme emotions in my life, never dreamed I could feel simultaneously heartbroken and euphoric," said Rowling.[1]

In October 2007, Rowling completed *The Tales of Beedle the Bard*, a volume of fairy tales that were mentioned in *Harry Potter and the Deathly Hallows*. Handwritten and illustrated by Rowling herself, and bound in leather and silver and inlaid with semiprecious stones, only seven copies of the book were printed. Rowling gave away six copies; the remaining volume was auctioned off for $3.9 million, with proceeds benefiting The Children's Voice, a charity.[2]

While Rowling says she has finished Harry's story and needs a break from writing about the wizarding world, she has not ruled out ever writing about Hogwarts again.

"I am not planning to do that," she said, "but I'm not going to say I'm never going to do it."[3]

More Controversy

While the initial controversy over the Harry Potter books seems to have calmed down, it is always possible that books involving the boy wizard will be challenged

121

or criticized again and that the final book will be used to support any argument against them.

After the case in Cedarville, Arkansas, where the court ruled that denying children access to Harry Potter books in the school library was a violation of their First Amendment rights, schools will probably not try to restrict access or out-and-out ban these or similar books, but they don't have to buy them, either. And teachers can be encouraged not to use them in the curriculum.

How Should Book Challenges Be Resolved?

There may always be parents who object to the teaching materials used at schools. One way schools may be able to prevent problems is to adopt a policy of notifying parents in advance as to what materials will be used in class during the school year. Parents could then ask that their children be transferred from a class in which Harry Potter—or any other reading material they object to—is part of the curriculum, or they could request an alternative reading assignment.

The nonprofit organization Citizens for Community Values/Family Friendly Libraries suggests that parents familiarize themselves with school libraries and communicate their concerns with teachers. If they do not want their child exposed to a particular book, they should write a letter requesting as much. Schools will generally be cooperative if parents express such concerns in writing.

"Parents need to work through the system if they find a book they don't want their child to read," said Phil Burress, president of Citizens for Community Values, which works to promote moral values in schools and in the community. "They should object only if their child is forced to read something they don't approve of and in that way they can serve as the collective moral conscience of the school."

Burress, who served on the Cincinnati Library Board for eight years, says it can reek of censorship if a parent asks that a book be removed from the school altogether. "It's only one person's opinion and everyone comes at it from a different point of view."

On the other hand, parents should not have to put up with their child's being forced to read a book that violates the moral standards and beliefs he or she is brought up with at home. If a child is forced to read a book that violates a family's beliefs, said Burress, parents are on solid ground when challenging school policy.

"School board members need to hear about that," said Burress. "Parents have the right to opt out of letting their child read anything controversial or anything they feel strongly against."

He suggests a cooperative approach. Getting angry is not productive. "It's better to study the issues, study the school's policies, find out what's going on, attend school board meetings, talk to teachers."

123

Another good idea is for parents to read the book themselves.

"If your child brings home a book you're not happy with, you need to read the book yourself to be sure and not rely on what other people have said," said Burress. "Oftentimes parents do not do their homework. They just hear about what's going on."[4]

Chris Finan of the American Booksellers Foundation for Free Expression agrees that parents have a right to ask for an alternative reading assignment if a book violates their beliefs, as long as the decision does not affect other people's children.

Finan, author of the book *The Fight for Free Speech,* helped to create the organization Muggles for Harry Potter when the book was removed from circulation in the Zeeland, Michigan, schools. Within a few months of creating the Muggles for Harry Potter Web site, he had received tens of thousands of e-mails requesting a copy of their newsletter.

"I was amazed at the amount of passion," said Finan. "Kids were outraged that anyone wanted to attack the books they loved."

For Finan, a defender of First Amendment rights, this was an exciting development, since many young people don't realize how the amendment can potentially affect their lives.

What can young readers do if a book they love or believe to be worthwhile is challenged, restricted, or banned in their school?

"They can circulate petitions, write letters to the local paper, the school newspaper. They can picket. They can hand out flyers, try to speak at school board meetings," said Finan. "Kids often do. I think that as long as parents approve, kids can participate in almost as many anti-censorship efforts as adults."

He also suggests getting help from organizations that deal with such issues, such as the National Coalition Against Censorship, the American Library Association, and the American Booksellers Foundation for Freedom of Expression.

"Kids can do anything from handing out a petition to becoming a plaintiff," said Finan.[5]

How to Challenge Books

There are several ways parents—or young people—can challenge books:

Express their concern verbally

Write a letter of complaint to the school or library

Publicly distribute information challenging the value of the printed material

Contact an organization such as Family Friendly Libraries/Citizens for Community Values or Parents Against Bad Books in Schools

When the teacher reached for *Harry Potter and the Sorcerer's Stone* in Eric Poliner's fifth-grade class, he left the room. Because his parents, born-again Christians, objected to the books, the fifth grader spent time in the hall reading another book. A student at Ledgeview Elementary School near Buffalo, New

How to Counter a Challenge

Parents—or young people— can counter a challenge by:

Voicing their concern to the school or library

Making a written complaint to the school or library

Attending a school board meeting

Filling out a Challenge Database form via the American Library Association

Contact the National Coalition Against Censorship or the American Booksellers Foundation for Free Expression

York, Eric felt left out at first, but said he then realized it was for his own good.

"There's a lot about witchcraft and evil and spells and magic," said Eric, age ten. "I was taught at church that that was not good."

Eric feels he learned a lot from his mother's protest of the book— and it is not just what you should or should not read.

"If they're doing something in schools that offends you or something," said Eric, "you can do something about it."[6]

That is also true for young readers who feel strongly about the worth of the books. It was the case for Dakota Counts, the fourth grader who, with her parents, protested restricted access to the Potter books in a Cedarville, Arkansas, school.

It was also true for a group of summer campers who called themselves the Fab Five. The five fifth-grade Texas girls—Rosalind, Lauren, Gretchen, Maura, and Elizabeth—became increasingly upset as they heard stories about Harry Potter books being banned even though the books had not been challenged in their school.

"I don't understand why parents and librarians who are trying to get us to read books in the library then ban books we want to read," said Lauren.

The girls organized a petition at camp and collected fifty signatures against banning the books. While they admitted that maybe there are some books a second grader should not read, they considered it a decision for parents and children to make together.[7]

Amanda Javaly (on left) and her friends attend a Harry Potter event at a local bookstore. Amanda has been reading the series since middle school.

Rowling agrees: "Of course parents have a perfect right to decide what their children see or read. I do not feel, however, that they have the right to decide what all of our children see and read. That's something different."[8]

For Amanda Javaly, seventeen, who has liked the books since middle school, the very fact the controversy exists makes it even more important that kids read the books.

"If kids have fought to be able to read the books that ought to tell you something," said Javaly. "If they're willing to fight for it, it's worth reading."[9]

And if kids fight to read the books and adults try to stop them, even more kids may want to read them.

Perhaps Rowling stated her opinion on this in *The Order of the Phoenix,* when she had Hermione say: "Oh, Harry, don't you see? If she [Professor Umbridge] could have done one thing to make absolutely sure that every single person in this school will read your interview, it was banning it!"[10]

Discussion Questions

1. Do the Harry Potter books make witchcraft seem appealing? If so, what parts of the idea of witchcraft are most appealing?

2. If you think you should be able to read Harry Potter books, what should the cutoff age be? Should a second grader be allowed to read Harry Potter? A fifth grader? Would you read a Harry Potter book to your little sister or to the boy you babysit for?

3. Are there other books or materials you think young kids should not read or see?

4. If you were a parent, how would you feel if a teacher or librarian decided what your children could or could not read?

5. What is Wicca? Do the Harry Potter books promote this religion? Why does this prospect upset so many people?

6. In your opinion, are the main characters in the Harry Potter books—Harry, Hermione, and Ron—good role models? Should readers try to be like them?

7. Do you know anyone, or have you heard of anyone, who was influenced to commit violence or disobey his or her parents because of something he or she read? If so, what was the reading material?

129

Timeline

This timeline covers book banning from the first book ever banned to the latest decisions, particularly those affecting the Harry Potter series:

387 B.C.—Plato suggests banning the *Iliad* and the *Odyssey* because of their potential bad influence on young people.

1450—Gutenberg invents the printing press in Germany, making it easier for the average person to read.

1470—First German office of censorship created.

1650—First publication in the United States banned because it contradicted accepted religious beliefs: *The Meritorious Price of Our Redemption.*

1873—Comstock Law passed.

1933—Nazis burn books in Germany.

1936—Parts of the Comstock Law declared unconstitutional.

1965—J. K. Rowling is born on July 31.

1975—*Island Trees* v. *Pico* case.

1982—Banned Books Week, sponsored by the American Library Association, is first celebrated nationally in the United States.

1997—*Harry Potter and the Philosopher's Stone* is published in Britain; published as *Harry Potter and the Sorcerer's Stone* in the United States.

1998—*Harry Potter and the Chamber of Secrets* is published.

1999—*Harry Potter and the Prisoner of Azkaban* is published.

130

—A parent at Simi Elementary School in Simi Valley asks school administrators to remove the book from the school curriculum. A committee of parents, teachers, and administrators reads the book and votes it can be read aloud.

—Superintendent Gary Feenstra of the Zeeland, Michigan, schools then places restrictions on reading, displaying, and borrowing *Harry Potter and the Sorcerer's Stone*.

2000—Parents Greg and Arlena Wilson ask school officials at Three Rivers Elementary School in Bend, Oregon, to ban all Harry Potter books from the school. The school board votes unanimously to keep the books.

—*Harry Potter and the Goblet of Fire* is published.

—Parents at the Orange Grove Elementary School in Whittier, California, request that all Harry Potter books be banned at the school. A district committee rejects their request.

—A parent asks the Arab, Alabama, Board of Education to remove the books from the school's libraries and curriculum. Three review committees recommend keeping the books, but teachers can make no recommendation requiring reading them.

—Parents in Franklin, Illinois, complain about the Harry Potter books to school district administrators. School officials decide not to censor the Harry Potter books.

—Santa Fe Independent School District in Texas requires written permission before students can check out any Harry Potter novels.

2002—In Cedarville, Arkansas, parents ask that the books be taken out of general circulation. The school board votes to place the books in a special library section and requires a signed permission slip before students can borrow them. A fourth-grade student, Dakota Counts, and her parents, Billy Ray Counts and Mary Nell Counts, sue the school to lift the restrictions. The district court rules that denying students access to the books violates their First Amendment rights.

2003—*Harry Potter and the Order of the Phoenix* is published.

2005—*Harry Potter and the Half-Blood Prince* is published.

2007—*Harry Potter and the Deathly Hallows* is published.

—*The Tales of Beedle the Bard* is published.

Chapter Notes

Chapter 1.
The Controversy Surrounding Harry Potter

1. Interview with Pilar Mendez-Cruz, July 15, 2005.

2. Ibid.

3. Interview with Amanda Javaly, July 15, 2005.

4. Interview with Lin Butter, July 15, 2005.

5. "'Evil' Harry Potter day canceled," BBC News, July 14, 2005, <http://bbc.co.uk/2/hi/uk_news/england/lincolnshire/4682519.stm> (July 15, 2005).

6. Harry R. Weber, "Ga. Judge: Keep Harry Potter Books in School," *The Christian Post*, May 30, 2007, <http://www.christianpost.com/article/2007 05 30/27682_Ga._Judge:_Keep_Harry_Potter_Books_in_ School.htm> (July 29, 2007).

7. Tamara Audi, "Church Group Burns Harry Potter Books, Shania Twain CDs," *Detroit Free Press*, August 6, 2003, p. 2B.

8. Ibid.

9. Sherry Thomas, "J.K. Rowling has the future mapped out for Harry Potter," *Houston Chronicle*, March 20, 2001, <http://www.quick-quote-quill.org/articles/2001/0301-houston-thomas.html> (May 30, 2006).

10. "Missouri Librarians Latest to Discover: Banning Makes Books Popular," *FreedomForum.org*, September 24, 2002, <http://www.freedomforum.org/

templates/document.asp?documentID=17008> (July 29, 2005).

11. Jeff Jensen, "Fire Storm," *Entertainment Weekly*, September 7, 2000, p. 11.

12. American Library Association, Office for Intellectual Freedom, *Intellectual Freedom Manual*, 6th ed. (Chicago: Western Publishing Company, 2002), pp. 156–157.

13. "Network Opposes Potter Policy," letter sent by National Coalition Against Censorship to *The Holland Sentinel*, April 19, 2000, <http://www.ncac.org/literature/20000419~USA~Zeeland_Public_Schools_Restrict_Harry_Potter_Books.cfm> (July 29, 2005).

14. Diane Weaver Dunne, "Look Out Harry Potter! Book Banning Heats Up," *Education World*, April 10, 2000, <www.educationworld.com/a_admin/admin/admin157.shtml> (May 31, 2006).

15. "Banned Books Week Kickoff Event Honors Muggles for Harry Potter," American Booksellers Foundation for Free Expression, September 21, 2000, <http://www.abffe.com/update2-9.htm> (July 29, 2005).

16. "Action Alerts," National Coalition Against Censorship, May 2000, <http://www.ncac.org/action/alertsarchive.cfm> (July 29, 2005).

17. "Back to School with the Religious Right," People For the American Way, n.d., <http://www.pfaw.org/pfaw/general/default.aspx?oid=3655> (July 29, 2005).

18. Julia Scheeres, "The Trouble With Harry Potter," *WiredNews*, November 15, 2001, <www.wired.com/news/culture/0,1284,48396,00.html> (July 29, 2005).

19. E-mail interview with anonymous PABBIS spokesperson, March 28, 2005.

Chapter 2.
Banned, Censored, and Bowdlerized

1. "Intellectual Freedom at Your Library," Joyner Library, East Carolina University, Greenville, North Carolina, n.d., <http://www.lib.ecu.edu/cdpgs/bbw2000.html> (April 14, 2005).

2. Jamie Allen, "Banned Books Week Spotlights Battle Over Censorship," *CNN*, September 27, 1999, <http://www.cnn.com/books/news/9909/27/bannedbooks> (July 29, 2005).

3. Ibid.

4. "Banned Books Resources," Central Connecticut State University, New Britain, Connecticut, n.d., <http://www.ccsu.edu/library/nadeau/Bibliographies/BannedBooks.htm> (July 29, 2005).

5. "Harry Potter Magically Reappears at Top of ALA's Most Challenged List," American Library Association, January 2003, <www.ala.org/ala/alonline/currentnews/newsarchive/2003/january2003/Default2565.htm> (March 14, 2005).

6. "Banned Books Online," University of Pennsylvania, n.d., <onlinebooks.library.upenn.edu/banned-books.html> (July 29, 2005).

7. Diane Ravitch, *The Language Police* (New York: Alfred A. Knopf, 2003), p. 84.

8. Ray Bradbury, *Fahrenheit 451* (New York: Ballantine Publishing Group, 1991), pp. 148–149.

9. Allen.

10. William Noble, *Bookbanning in America* (Middlebury, Vt.: Paul S. Eriksson, 1990), p. xxii.

11. "Another Springfield First, " Springfield Library, n.d., <http://www.springfieldlibrary.org/Pynchon/pynchon.html> (July 29, 2005).

12. Ravitch, p. 71.

13. Heinrich Heine, *Almansor: A Tragedy*, 1821, <http://www.ala.org/ala/oif/bannedbooksweek/bookburning/20thcentury/nazigermany/nazigermany.htm> (June 1, 2006)

14. 'The Most Frequently Challenged Books of 1990–2000," American Library Association. n.d., <www.ala.org/ala/oif/bannedbooksweek/bbwlink/100mostfrequently.htm> (February 8, 2005).

15. Kris Adams Wendt, "Reading Between the Lines," Rhinelander Public Library Web site, September 26, 2004, <http://wvls.lib.wi.us/RhinelanderDistrictLibrary/2004%20Columns/banned_books.htm> (March 15, 2005).

16. Claire Mullally, "Banned Books: Overview," First Amendment Center, n.d., <http://www.firstamendmentcenter.org/speech/libraries/topic.aspx?topic=banned_books> (April 17, 2005).

17. Ibid.

18. Robert D. Stone, "School Libraries and the First Amendment: An Analysis of Island Trees," a bound report by Legal Affairs State Education Department, New York, August 6, 1982, p. 3.

19. Barbara Parker and Stefanie Weiss, *An Activist's Guide to Protecting the Freedom to Learn* (Washington, D.C.: People For the American Way, 1994).

20. "Mark Twain's Letters 1876–1885," *Classic Literature Library*, n.d., <http://mark-twain.classic literature.co.uk/mark-twains-letters-1876-1885/ebook-page-85.asp> (August 28, 2005).

Chapter 3.
J. K. Rowling: A Life Worthy of a Novel

1. J. K. Rowling on the Diane Rehm show, WAMU 88.5 FM, *The Quick Quote Quill*, December 24, 1999, <www.quick-quote-quill.org/articles/1999/1299-wamu-rehm.htm> (May 31, 2006).

2. "Biography," *J.K. Rowling Web site*, n.d., <http://www.JKRowling.com> (July 29, 2005)

3. Lindsey Fraser, *An Interview with JK Rowling* (London: Mammoth/Egmont Children's Books, 2000), p 1.

4. "Biography," *J.K. Rowling Web site*.

5. Connie Ann Kirk, *J. K. Rowling: A Biography* (Westport, Conn.: Greenwood Press, 2003), p. 13.

6. Fraser, p. 7.

7. Ibid., p. 19.

8. "Biography," J. K. Rowling Web site.

9. "Transcript of J. K. Rowling's Live Interview on Scholastic.com," *Scholastic online*, February 3, 2000, <www.scholastic.com/harrypotter/author/transcript1.htm> (March 25, 2005).

10. Kirk, p. 67.

11. Malcolm Jones, "Why Harry's Hot," *Newsweek*, July 17, 2000, p. 56.

12. Fraser, p. 25.

13. "Potter author names baby daughter," *BBC News online*, January 25, 2005, <http://news.bbc.co.uk/2/hi/entertainment/arts/4206787.stm> (August 15, 2005).

14. Peter Griffiths, "Potter Fans Beg Rowling to Save Harry," *Yahoo! News*, July 9, 2007, <http://news.yahoo.com/s/nm/20070709/en_nm/britain_potter_dc> (July 29, 2007).

15. "Rowling 'heartbroken, euphoric' as Potter ends," *MSNBC*, February 6, 2007, <http://www.msnbc.msn.com/id/17008981> (July 29, 2007).

16. Jen Brown, "J.K. Rowling Brings Meredith Vieira to Tears," *MSNBC*, July 26, 2007, <http://allday.msnbc.msn.com/archive/2007/07/26/288781.aspx> (July 29, 2007).

17. Carol Memmott, "JK Rowling's Fond Look Back At Harry Potter," *USA Today*, July 25, 2007, <http://www.usatoday.com/life/books/news/2007-07-25-jk-rowling_N.htm> (July 29, 2007).

Chapter 4.
The Secrets Behind The Sorcerer's Stone

1. Margaret Weir, "Of magic and single mother-hood," *Salon.com*, March 31, 1999, <http://www.salon.com/mwt/feature/1999/03cov_31featureb.html> (June 1, 2006).

2. Mary Pharr, "In Medias Res: Harry Potter As Hero-in-Progress," in Lana A. Whited, ed., *The Ivory Tower and Harry Potter* (Columbia, Mo.: University of Missouri Press, 2002), p. 54.

3. Edmund M. Kern, *The Wisdom of Harry Potter* (Amherst, N.Y.: Prometheus Books, 2003), p. 54.

4. Bruno Bettelheim, *The Uses of Enchantment* (New York: Vintage, 1989), p. 5.

Chapter 5.
Potter Power

1. "Harry Potter posts spellbinding sales," *CNNMoney.com*, July 23, 2007, <http://money.cnn.com/2007/07/23/news/companies/scholastic_potter/index.htm> (November 23, 2007).

2. "Potter fans snap up latest book," *BBC News*, July 16, 2005, <http://news.bbc.co.uk/2/hi/entertainment/4683503.stm> (May 31, 2006)

3. "A magical day for Harry Potter fans," *CNN*, July 16, 2005, <http://www.cnn.com/2005/SHOWBIZ/books/07/16/launching.harry> (July 16, 2005).

4. "Harry Potter and the Half-Blood Prince," *Movie Magic*, July 2005, p. 8.

5. Edmund M. Kern, *The Wisdom of Harry Potter* (Amherst, N.Y.: Prometheus Books, 2003), p. 62.

6. Ibid, pp. 73–74.

7. Steven R, Weisman, "A Novel That Is a Midsummer's Night Dream," editorial, *The New York Times*, July 11, 2000, Section A, p. 24; and "Great Books About Depression," *PBS Kids.org*, <http://pbskids.org/itsmylife/emotions/depression/print_books.html> (July 29, 2005).

8. Sandra Martin, "Out of Adversity Harry Was Born," *The* (Toronto) *Globe Review*, October 23, 2000, <http://www.quick-quote-quill.org/articles/2000/1000-globereview-martin.html> (April 13, 2006).

Chapter 6.
Potter's World Becomes Even Darker

1. Edmund M. Kern, *The Wisdom of Harry Potter* (Amherst, N.Y.: Prometheus Books, 2003), pp. 86–87.

2. Lindsey Fraser, *An Interview with JK Rowling* (London: Mammoth/Egmont Children's Books, 2000), p. 49.

3. Malcolm Jones "Why Harry's Hot," *Newsweek*, July 17, 2000, p. 56.

4. Mary Pharr, "In Medias Res: Harry Potter as Hero-in-Progress," in Lana A. Whited, ed., *The Ivory Tower and Harry Potter* (Columbia, Mo.: University of Missouri Press, 2002), p. 65.

5. J. K. Rowling radio interview with Evan Solomon/Radio Canada, *CBC News World*, n.d., <http://

www.cbc.ca/programs/sites/hottype_rowlingcomplete
.html> (July 29, 2005).

6. "Rowling's tears at Potter book death," *BBC News*, June 18, 2003, <http://news.bbc.co.uk/2/hi/entertainment/2998198.stm> (June 25, 2005).

7. M. Katherine Grimes, "Harry Potter: Fairy Tale Prince, Real Boy, and Archetypal Hero," in Lana A. Whited, ed., *The Ivory Tower and Harry Potter* (Columbia, Mo.: University of Missouri Press, 2002), p. 101.

8. Heather Chapman, "Adult Issues Take Series to Next Level," *Lexington Herald-Leader*, July 19, 2005, p. D1.

9. Lev Grossman, "J. K. Rowling Hogwarts and All," *Time*, July 25, 2005, p. 64.

10. Barbara F. Meltz, "Young Potter readers need to talk, grieve," *The Boston Globe*, July 21, 2005, <http://www.boston.com/yourlife/home/articles/2005/07/21/young_potter_readers_need_to_talk_grieve/> (July 21, 2005).

11. Ibid.

12. Deepti Hajela, "A dark 'Prince' marks turning point for Potter," Associated Press, July 16, 2005, <http://www.msnbc.msn.com/id/8587703/> (July 22, 2005).

13. Mary Carle McCauley, "An inevitable ending to the Harry Potter Series," *Baltimore Sun*, July 18, 2007, <http://www.baltimoresun.com/entertainment/books

mags/bal-2potter0718,0,2741335.story> (July 18, 2007).

14. Elizabeth Hand, "Harry's Final Fantasy: Last Time's the Charm," *Washington Post*, July 22, 2007, <http://www.washingtonpost.com/wp-dyn/content/article/2007/07/21/AR2007072101025.html> (August 5, 2007).

15. "A generation says goodbye to Harry Potter," *CNN.com*, July 24, 2007, <http://www.cnn.com/2007/US/07/23/potter.generation.ap/index.html> (August 5, 2007).

16. Ibid.

17. Jacqueline Blais, "Harry Potter and the Deathly Hallows is a literal page-turner," *USA Today*, July 22, 2007, <http://www.usatoday.com/life/books/news/2007-07-22-potter-cover_N.htm> (August 5, 2007).

Chapter 7.
Challenging Harry Potter

1. "Harry Potter series again tops list of most challenged books," American Library Association, news release, January 2001, <http://www.ala.org/Template.cfm?Section=archive&template=/contentmanagement/contentdisplay.cfm&ContentID=7222> (June 1, 2006).

2. "Is Harry Potter A Harmless Fantasy Or Wicca Training Program?" Traditional Values Coalition, n.d., <http://www.traditionalvalues.org/modules.php?sid=144> (July 5, 2005).

3. Herbert Foerstel, *Banned in the U.S.A.* (Westport, Conn.: Greenwood Press, 2002), p. 185.

4. "Oregon School District Votes to Keep Harry Potter," *ALA News Briefs*, February 28, 2000, <http://archive.ala.org/alonline/news/2000/000228.html> (July 25, 2005).

5. "Wiccans dispute Potter Claims," Atlanta Christian Apologetics Project, October 25, 2000, <http://www.apologeticsindex.org/news/an201026.html#15> (July 24, 2005).

6. "Back to School with the Religious Right," People For the American Way, n.d., <http://www.pfaw.org/pfaw/general/default.aspx?oid=3655> (August 4, 2005).

7. Daniel Eaton, "The Harry Potter Controversy: Does Harry Potter Promote Witchcraft or the Occult?" Atlanta Christian Apologetics Project, n.d., <http://www.atlantaapologist.org/harrypotter.html> (August 4, 2005).

8. "Evil Harry Potter Attacked by Parents," *BBC News: Education*, October 13, 1999, <http://news.bbc.co.uk/1/hi/education/473513.stm> (June 1, 2006).

9. Martin Savidge, "Bubbling troubles trail Harry," *CNN*, July 6, 2000, <http://archives.cnn.com/2000/books/news/07/06/trouble.harry> (August 16, 2005).

10. "Parents call for ban on Harry Potter," *American School Board Journal*, December 1999, <http://

www.asbj.com/199912/1299beforetheboard.html>
(August 17, 2005).

11. "Banned Books Week: Join TLC in the Fight For Free Speech," *The Leaky Cauldron*, September 24, 2004, <http://www.the-leaky-cauldron.org/MTarchives/week_2004_09_19.html> (July 4, 2005).

12. Ben Ehrenreich, "The Wizard of Simi: Harry Potter's magic survived another match with Muggles-parents," *LAWeekly*, November 19–25, 1999, <http://www.laweekly.com/news/news/the-wizard-of-simi/6171/> (April 17, 2006).

13. Foerstel, p. 186.

14. "Zeeland School Board Won't Oppose Anti-Potter Order," *ALA News Briefs*, February 28, 2000, <http://archive.ala.org/alonline/news/2000/000228.html> (August 12, 2005).

15. "ABFFE, Seven Groups Announce Formation of Muggles for Harry Potter," American Booksellers Foundation For Free Expression, *ABFFE Update*, March 8, 2000, <http://www.abffe.com/update2-3.htm> (August 14, 2005).

16. American Library *Organization, Office of Intellectual Freedom Newsletter*, March 2000.

17. "The Brechner Report: April 2000," Brechner Center for Freedom of Information, College of Journalism and Communications, <http://brechner.org/reports/2000/04apr2000.pdf> (July 5, 2005).

18. Foerstel, p. 185.

19. Robert P. Doyle, "Books Challenged or Banned 2000–2001," Center for the Book of the Library of Congress, n.d., <https://www.ila.org/pdf/2005banned.pdf> (July 5, 2005).

20. Foerstel, pp. 185–186.

21. American Library Association, *Office of Intellectual Freedom Newsletter*, May 2000.

22. "Alabama School District Votes To Keep Harry Potter," American Library Association, December 25, 2000, <www.ala.org/al_onlineTemplate.cfm?Section=december2000&Template=/ContentManagement/ContentDisplay.cfm&ContentID=5068> (July 5, 2005).

23. "Texas School District: No 'Harry Potter' Without Parental OK," *FreedomForum.org*, October 6, 2000, <http://www.freedomforum.org/templates/document.asp?documentID=3251> (July 9, 2005).

24. Foerstel, p. 188.

25. "Missouri Librarians Latest To Discover: Banning Makes Books Popular," First Amendment Center, September 24, 2002, <http://www.freedomforum.org/templates/document.asp?documentID=17008> (July 5, 2005).

26. "Harry Potter Lawsuit Edges Closer to Court," American Library Association, March 10, 2003, <www.cfif.org/htdocs/legal_issues/legal_updates/first_amendment_cases/harry_potter.htm> (July 9, 2005).

27. "Justice, Not Magic, Returns Harry Potter Series to Library Bookshelves," Center for Individual

Freedom, April 24, 2003, <http://www.cfif.org/htdocs/legal_issues/legal_updates/first_amendment_cases/harry_potter.htm> (July 19, 2005).

28. "Judge Smites Harry Potter Restrictions in Arkansas," American Library Association, April 28, 2003, <www.ala.org/ala/alonline/currentnews/newsarchive/2003/april2003/judgesmitesharry.htm> (July 9, 2005).

29. Jim Hickey, "Book Ban Petition to Be Heard," *Middletown Press*, August 27, 2002, <http://www.zwire.com/site/news.cfm?newsid=5166014&BRD=1645&PAG=461&dept_id=10856&rfi=6> (July 10, 2005).

30. Laura Mallory, "GA Harry Potter Case - Myth v. Truth," *His Voice Today*, 2007, <http://www.hisvoicetoday.org/mythtruth.htm> (August 5, 2007).

31. Ibid.

32. "Harry Potter Books Banned in Rockford Catholic School," American Library Association, August 28, 2000, <http://archive.ala.org/alonline/news/2000/000828.html> (July 10, 2005).

33. Lana A. Whited, "Harry Potter: From Craze to Classic?" in Lana A. Whited, ed., *The Ivory Tower and Harry Potter* (Columbia, Mo.: University of Missouri Press, 2002), p. 3.

34. Catherine Shanahan, "Distinguishing good from evil earns Harry Papal honour," *Irish Examiner*, February 5, 2003, <http://archives.tcm.ie/irish examiner/2003/02/05story786988783> (July 10, 2005).

35. Rhys Blakely, "Pope criticizes Harry Potter," *The Sunday Times (U.K.)*, July 13, 2005, <http://www.timesonline.co.uk/article/o,,1-1692341,00.html>

36. Ehrenreich.

37. "Harry Potter Spooks Oskaloosa, Kansas," American Library Association, June 18, 2001, <http://www.ala.org/alaonlineTemplate.cfm?Section=june2001&Template=/ContentManagement/ContentDisplay.cfm&ContentID=7276> (July 10, 2005).

38. "Jacksonville Library Drops Harry Potter Certificates," American Library Association, September 18, 2000, <www.ala.org/ala/alonline/currentnews/newsarchive/2000/september2000/Default1080.htm> (May 31, 2006)

39. "Potter Books Cause Stir in Pennsylvania Town," *FreedomForum.org*, January 24, 2002, <http://www.freedomforum.org/templates/document.asp?documentID=15657> (July 15, 2005).

40. "Back To School With the Religious Right," People For the American Way, n.d., <http://www.pfaw.org/pfaw/general/default.aspx?oid=3655> (July 15, 2005).

41. "'Satanic' Harry Potter Books Burnt," *BBC News*, December 31, 2001, <http://news.bbc.co.uk/1/hi/entertainment/arts/1735623.stm> (July 15, 2005).

42. Indiana Department of Education, "Quarterly Report," January-March 2003, p. 2 <http://www.

doe.state.in.us/legal/pdf/quarterly_reports/2003_
janmar_v2.pdf> (May 31, 2006)

43. Tamara Audi, "Church Group Burns Harry
Potter Books, Shania Twain CDs," *Detroit Free Press*,
August 6, 2003, p. 2B.

44. Gregory Rice, "Book Cutting," *Sun Journal*
(Lewiston, Maine), November 15, 2001, p. 1.

45. Shanahan.

Chapter 8.
Does Harry Potter Matter?

1. Interview with Tamara Stewart, July 14, 2005.

2. David Smith, "Potter's Magic Spell Turns Boys
Into Bookworms," July 10, 2005, <http://books
.guardian.co.uk/harrypotter/story/0,,1525488,00>
(July 16, 2005).

3. Larry King Live interview, October 2000,
reprinted www.Mugglenet.com, July 5, 2005.

4. Katie Couric *Dateline NBC* Interview with J. K.
Rowling, "Inside 'Order of the Phoenix,'" December 8,
2003, <http://www.msnbc.com/id/3080035> (July 29,
2005).

5. Sherry Thomas, "JK Rowling Has The Future
Mapped Out for Harry Potter," *Houston Chronicle*,
March 20, 2001, <http://www.quick-quote-quill.org/
articles/2001/0301-houston-thomas.html> (May 30,
2006).

6. Judy Blume, "Is Harry Potter Evil?" *The New York Times*, October 22, 1999, p. A27.

7. Connie Neal, *What's a Christian to Do With Harry Potter?* (Colorado Springs, Colo.: Waterbrook Press, 2001), p. 37.

8. Dave Kopel, "Mugglemania," *The National Review*, July 22, 2000, <http://davekopel.org/NRO/2000/mugglemania.htm> (July 22, 2005).

9. "Forbidden Library: Banned and Challenged Books," *Amazon.com*, n.d., <http://author.forbiddenlibrary.com/> (July 16, 2005).

10. C. S. Lewis, *Of Other Worlds* (Bakersfield, Calif.: Harcourt Trade Publishers, 1975), p. 24.

11. Gregory Maguire, "Lord of the Golden Snitch," *The New York Times*, September, 5, 1999, <http://query.nytimes.com/gst/fullpage.html?res=9E0DE0D7173BF936A3575AC0A96F958260> (July 29, 2005)

12. Chris Armstrong, "Christian History Corner: Saint J.R.R. The Evangelist," March 1, 2003, <http://ctlibrary.com> (May 31, 2006)

13. *In The Shadow of the Wizard: Literature Challenged: A Bibliography*, University of Delaware Library, n.d., <http://www2.lib.udel.edu/subj/lgst/resguide/wizardex/wizardbib.htm> (July 16, 2005).

14. Neal, p. 78.

15. Ibid., pp. 73–74.

16. Lisa Jackson, "The Return of Harry Potter," *Christianity Today.com*, October 2000, <http://www.christianitytoday.com/cpt/2000/005/4.44.html> (July 29, 2005).

17. John Killinger, *God, the Devil, and Harry Potter* (New York: St. Martin's Press, 2002), pp. 81, 160.

18. Ibid, p. 186.

19. Nancy Churnin, "Christian Opposition to Harry Softens," *The Miami Herald*, July 23, 2005, <www.miami.com/mld/miamiherald/2005/07/23/living/12194767.htm> (May 31, 2006).

20. Bob Smietana, "The Gospel According to JK Rowling," *Christianity Today*, July 23, 2007, <http://www.christianitytoday.com/ct/2007/julyweb-only/130-12.0.html> (July 24, 2007).

21. Kevin Jackson, "Final Harry Potter Hits Shelves—As a Christian Tale," *The Christian Post*, July 21, 2007, <http://www.christianpost.com/article/20070721/28547_Final_'Harry_Potter'_Hits_Shelves_%85_as_a_Christian_Tale%3F.htm> (July 24, 2007).

22. Jan Glidewell, "Wiccans Are Not All That Wild About Harry Potter," *St. Petersburg Times*, January 16, 2001, reprinted Center for Studies of New Religion Web site, <www.cesnur.org/2001/potter/nov_12.htm> (July 28, 2005).

23. Marysia Kolodziej, "Harry Potter: The Witch's View," *BBC News*, June 23, 2003, <http://

news.bbc.co.uk/1/hi/entertainment/arts/3012270.stm> (July 28, 2005).

24. Edmund M. Kern, *The Wisdom of Harry Potter* (Amherst, N.Y.: Prometheus Books, 2003), p. 150.

25. Christine Schoefer, "Harry Potter's Girl Trouble," *Salon.com*, January 13, 2000, <www.salon.com/books/feature/2000/01/13/potter> (July 28, 2005).

26. Eliza T. Dresang, "Hermione Granger and the Heritage of Gender," in Lana A. Whited, ed., *The Ivory Tower and Harry Potter* (Columbia, Mo.: University of Missouri Press, 2002), p. 220.

27. Ibid, p. 223.

28. "JK Rowling Expecting Baby," *BBC News online*, September 20, 2002, <http://news.bbc.co.uk/1/hi/entertainment/showbiz/2269818.stm> (August 2, 2005).

29. Anthony Holden, "Why Harry Potter Doesn't Cast a Spell Over Me," *Guardian Unlimited*, June 25, 2000, <http://observer.guardian.co.uk/review/story/0,6903,335923,00.html> (August 2, 2005).

30. Harold Bloom, "Can 35 Million Book Buyers Be Wrong? Yes." *The Wall Street Journal*, July 11, 2000, <http://wrt-brooke.syr.edu/courses/205.03/bloom.html> (August 2, 2005).

Chapter 9.
Breaking the Spell: Ending the Harry Potter Series

1. "Rowling 'heartbroken, euphoric' as Potter ends," *MSNBC*, February 6, 2007, <http:

//www.msnbc.msn.com/id/17008981/>   (July   30, 2007).

2. "Amazon buys Rowling book for nearly $4 million," *msn.com*, December 13, 2007, <http://www.msnbc.msn.com/id/22240285/?GT1=10645> (December 14, 2007).

3. "Rowling: Harry's story comes to a definite end," *MSNBC*, July 19, 2007, <http://www.msnbc.msn.com/id/19850371/> (August 5, 2007).

4. Interview with Phil Burress, Citizens for Community Values, August 26, 2005.

5. Interview with Chris Finan, American Booksellers Foundation for Free Expression, August 29, 2005.

6. Jodi Wilgoren, "Don't Give Us Little Wizards, the Anti-Potter Parents Cry," *The New York Times*, November 1, 1999, p. 1.

7. Tiffany Durham, "Fab Five: Freedom of Speech Fighters for Harry Potter!" *American Booksellers Association Web site*, n.d., <http://www.booksense.com/readup/themes/harrykids.jsp> (August 21, 2005).

8. J. K. Rowling interview on The Diane Rehm Show, WAMU Radio, Washington, D.C., *The Quick Quote Quill*, December 24, 1999, <www.quick-quote-quill.org/articles/1999/1299-wamu-rehm.htm> (May 31, 2006)

9. Interview with Amanda Javaly, July 15, 2005.

10. J. K. Rowling, *Harry Potter and the Order of the Phoenix* (New York: Arthur A Levine Books, 2003), p. 582.

Published works of J. K. Rowling

1997 *Harry Potter and the Philosopher's Stone*
(U.S. title: *Harry Potter and the Sorcerer's Stone*)

1998 *Harry Potter and the Chamber of Secrets*

1999 *Harry Potter and the Prisoner of Azkaban*

2000 *Harry Potter and the Goblet of Fire*

2001 *Fantastic Beast and Where to Find Them*

2001 *Quidditch Through the Ages*

2003 *Harry Potter and the Order of the Phoenix*

2005 *Harry Potter and the Half-Blood Prince*

2007 *Harry Potter and the Deathly Hallows*
The Tales of Beedle the Bard

Glossary

abridging—Shortening, reducing in length.

Azkaban—The wizard prison featured in the Harry Potter books.

Dark Mark—The symbol of the Death Eaters, consisting of a green skull with a serpent's tongue.

Death Eater—A supporter of Voldemort.

Dementors—Cloaked figures that suck out the souls of their victims; guards at Azkaban.

gender stereotyping—Assigning characteristics to a person based on what you think a person of that gender should be doing.

gratuitous—Unnecessary; serving no purpose.

Horcrux—An object containing part of a person's soul.

litany—A prayer used in a religious service, consisting of a series of repeated phrases.

Mattachine—Relating to the Mattachine Society of New York, an early gay-rights organization.

Mudblood—A highly offensive term for a witch or wizard whose parents are Muggles.

Muggle—A human being with no magical blood.

Parselmouth—The language of snakes, which some wizards can speak.

154

Glossary

Patronus—A silvery image of an animal produced by a witch or wizard's positive emotions; a defense against Dementors.

pedestrian—Lacking wit or imagination.

Portkey—A commonplace object that transports those who touch it to another place.

Quidditch—A game played in the air on broomsticks.

redress—To take action against, compensate, or correct.

satanism—The worship of devils.

Snitch—A winged gold ball used in Quidditch.

Time-Turner—A magical device that allows the user to go back in time.

triathlon—An athletic competition consisting of three consecutive events.

Wicca—A polytheistic, nature-based religion associated with witchcraft and based on pre-Christian traditions.

Women's Lib—Short for Women's Liberation, a movement seeking equal rights for women.

wraith—A spirit; a thin, pale figure.

For More Information

American Civil Liberties Union
125 Broad Street, 18th Floor
New York, NY 10004

American Library Association
50 E. Huron Street
Chicago, IL 60611
1-800-545-2433

Christian Broadcasting Network
977 Centerville Turnpike
Virginia Beach, VA 23463
(757) 226-7000

Christian Coalition of America
P.O. Box 37030
Washington, DC 20013-7030
(202) 479-6900

Concerned Women for America
1015 Fifteenth Street, NW,
Suite 1100
Washington, DC 20005
(202) 488-7000

Family Friendly
Libraries/Citizens for
Community Values
11175 Reading Road, Suite 103
Cincinnati, OH 45241
(513) 733-5775

Focus on the Family
8605 Explorer Drive
Colorado Springs, CO 80920
1-800-A-FAMILY (232-6459)

National Campaign for Freedom
of Expression
1736 Franklin Street, 9th Floor
Oakland, CA 94612
(510) 208-7744

National Coalition Against
Censorship
275 Seventh Avenue
New York, NY 1001
(212) 807-6222

People for the American Way
2000 M Street, NW, Suite 400
Washington, DC 20036
(202) 467-4999
1-800-326-7329

Further Reading

Books

Beahm, George. *Fact, Fiction, and Folklore in Harry Potter's World: An Unofficial Guide*. Charlottesville, Va.: Hampton Roads Publishing Co., 2005.

Boyle, Fiona. *A Muggle's Guide to the Wizarding World: Exploring the Harry Potter Universe*. Toronto: ECW Press, 2004.

Chippendale, Lisa A. *Triumph of the Imagination: The Story of Writer J. K. Rowling*. Philadelphia: Chelsea House, 2002.

Karolides, Nicholas J., Margaret Bald, and Dawn B. Sova. *100 Banned Books: Censorship Histories of World Literature*. New York: Checkmark Books/Facts On File, 1999.

Kirk, Connie Ann. *JK Rowling: A Biography*. Westport, Conn.: Greenwood Publishing Group, 2003.

Weiner, Gary, editor. *Readings on J. K. Rowling*. San Diego: Greenhaven Press, 2003.

Internet Addresses

American Library Association
  <http://www.ala.org>

The J. K. Rowling Web site
  <http://www.JKRowling.com>

Family Friendly Libraries
  <http://www.fflibraries.org>

Index

158

Index